TEHACHAPI PRISON WEDDING: MAY 1976

Eric "Superman" Sturgess

Rose Of Sharon
PUBLISHING

ERIC "SUPERMAN" STURGESS

Printed Worldwide
First Printing 2025
First Edition 2025

10 9 8 7 6 5 4 3 2 1

Rose of Sharon Publishing books may be ordered through booksellers or by contacting:

Rose Of Sharon Publishing
roseofsharonpublishing.com
P.O. Box 186
Floresville, Texas 78114

ISBN:978-1-970335-13-2 Paperback

Preface

The wedding photos feature Robert Jackson and his wife, Jo Ann, during a visit at Tehachapi State Prison in California. Their wedding was on May 27, 1976, inside the visiting area of the prison. Inmates in the state of California are allowed to get married in prison. During this time, prisoners in the California Department of Corrections were allowed to wear their personal clothes to visits.

Robert and Jo Ann were featured in an article in the San Francisco Chronicle on May 28, 1976, titled "The Brides of Folsom Prison." He was incarcerated in these photos in the book from 1976 through 1980. He was also at several state prisons, including Folsom, California Men's Colony, Chino, and Tehachapi.

These photos are a snapshot of time that captures Robert doing his best to survive behind those cold prison walls. These photos and the people in them deserve to be seen by others and their lives not forgotten in the dustbins of history. It just reminds us how fleeting our lives are. Nobody is guaranteed tomorrow, and our youth quickly fades to old age in the blink of an eye.

God bless you
Eric Sturgess
Romans 10:9-13

Table of Contents

Introduction

The photographs of Robert Jackson and his wife, Jo Ann, capture a rare and deeply human moment within the walls of Tehachapi State Prison in California. Their wedding took place on May 27, 1976, inside the visiting area—an unlikely setting for such a sacred event, yet filled with the same joy, hope, and devotion that define every marriage. During this era, inmates in the California Department of Corrections were permitted to marry and, notably, allowed to wear their own personal clothing during visits. This simple privilege added a faint sense of normalcy to a life otherwise bound by the routines and restrictions of incarceration.

Robert and Jo Ann's story reached beyond prison walls when they were featured in the San Francisco Chronicle on May 28, 1976, in an article titled "The Brides of Folsom Prison." The piece chronicled the resilience of love and commitment that persisted even in confinement. Robert was incarcerated from 1976 through 1980, serving time in several state prisons, including Folsom, the California Men's Colony, Chino, and Tehachapi. Each of these institutions left its mark, yet these images from those prisons—quiet moments between husband and wife—reveal a side of prison life rarely seen: tenderness, endurance, and humanity behind the razor wire.

These photographs are more than documentation—they are time capsules. They show Robert not as an inmate number, but as a man doing his best to survive behind cold concrete walls, clinging to connection and dignity. The images remind us that every person, regardless of circumstance, has a story that deserves to be remembered.

Many of these lives have faded into history, their faces now long forgotten. But here, preserved in these pages, their stories breathe again. These photos testify to love's persistence, to the fragility of time, and to the unshakable truth that even within the hardest places, moments of beauty and grace still exist.

Life moves swiftly—youth turns to age, joy to memory. Nobody is promised tomorrow. These photographs, frozen in 1976, invite us to pause and remember: every life, every story, and every moment matters.

Photographs

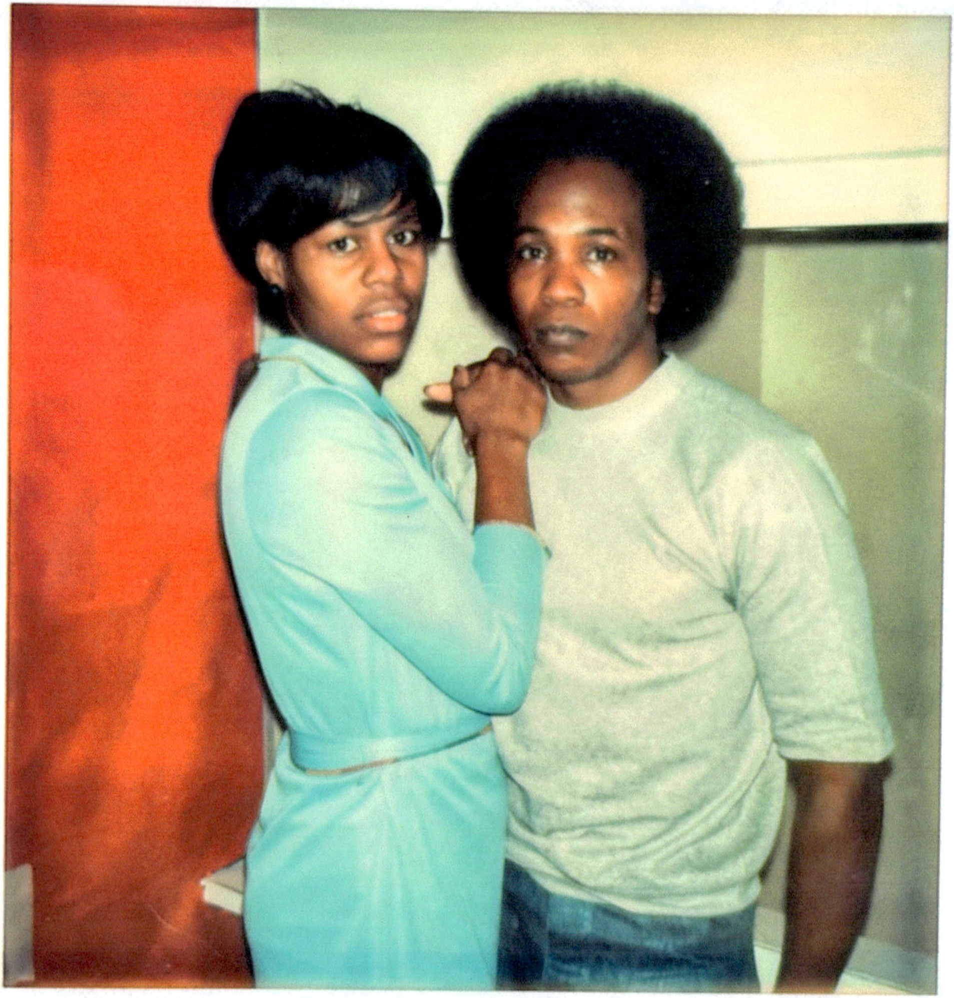

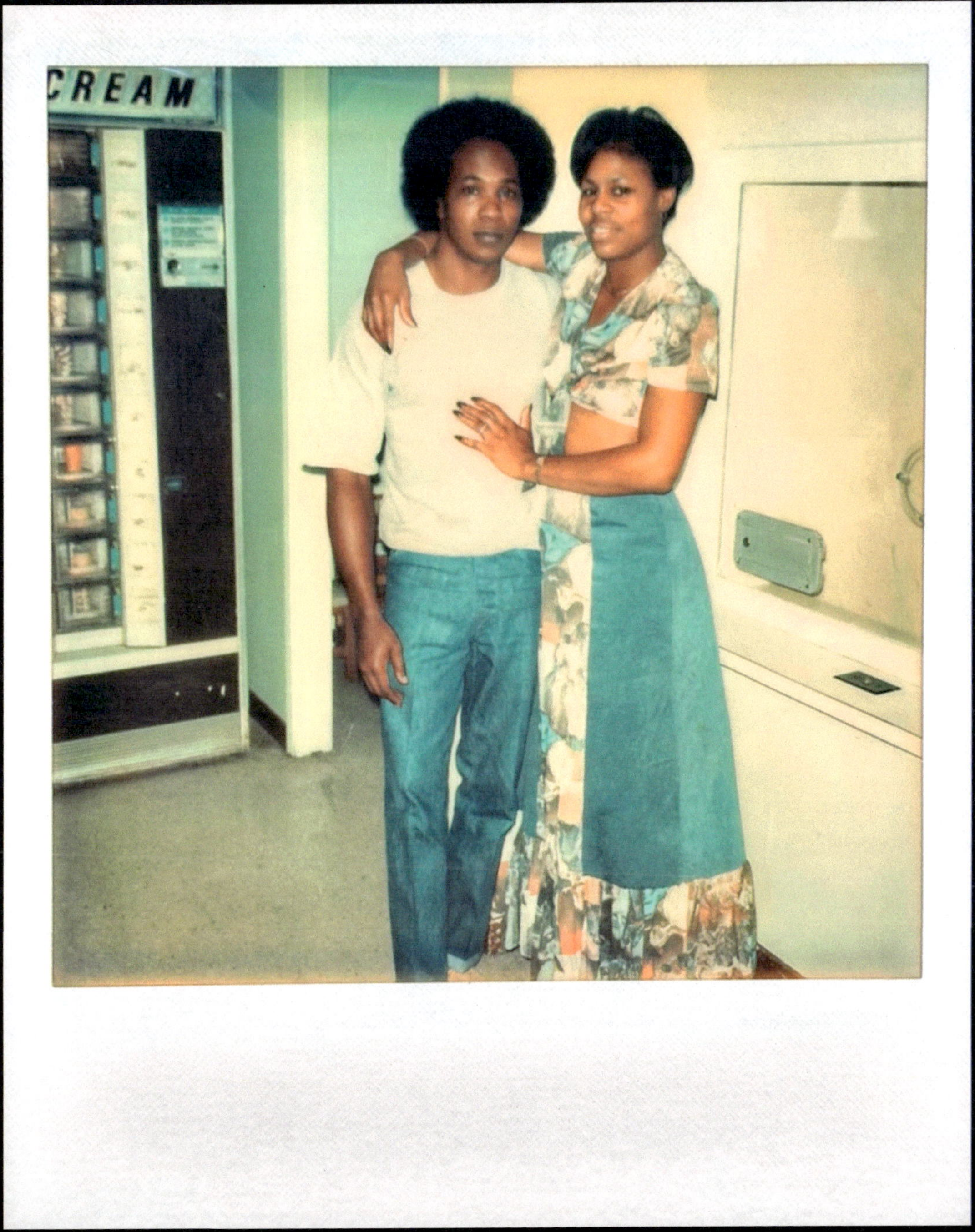

s picture was taken in the visiting area of Tehachapi State Prison on January 18, 1976

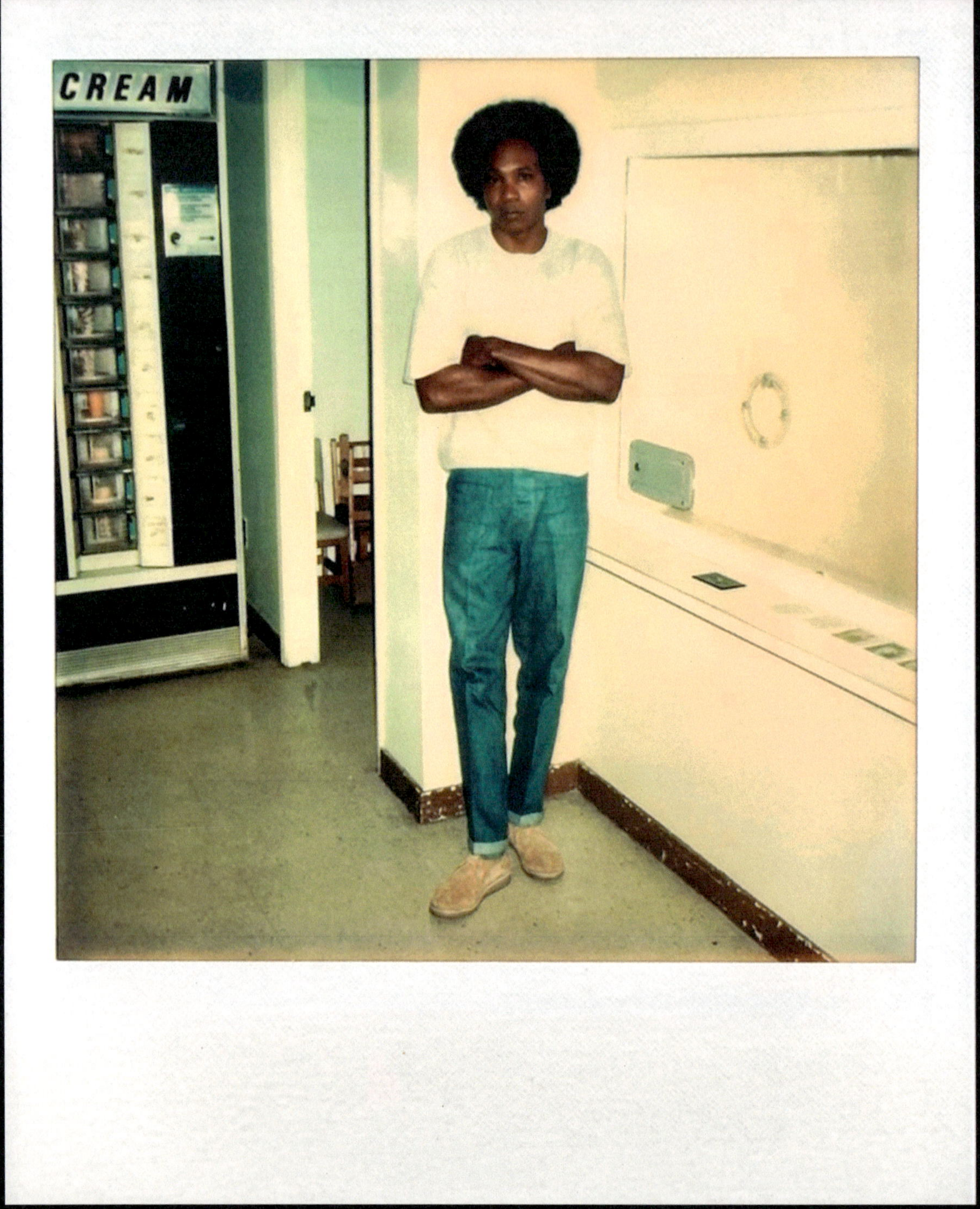

This picture was taken in the visiting area of Tehachapi State Prison on January 18, 1976.

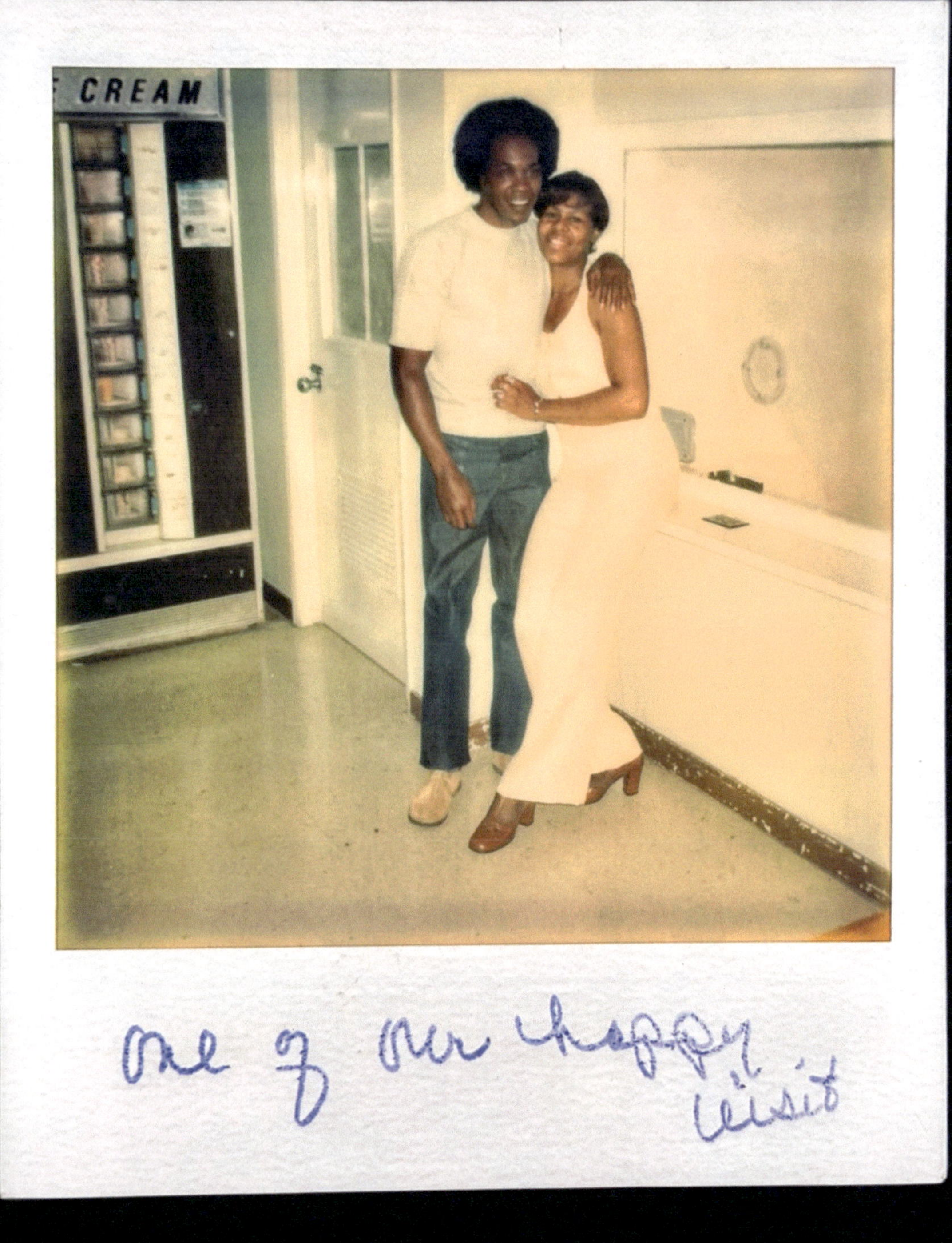

is picture was taken in the visiting area of Tehachapi State Prison on May 9, 1976

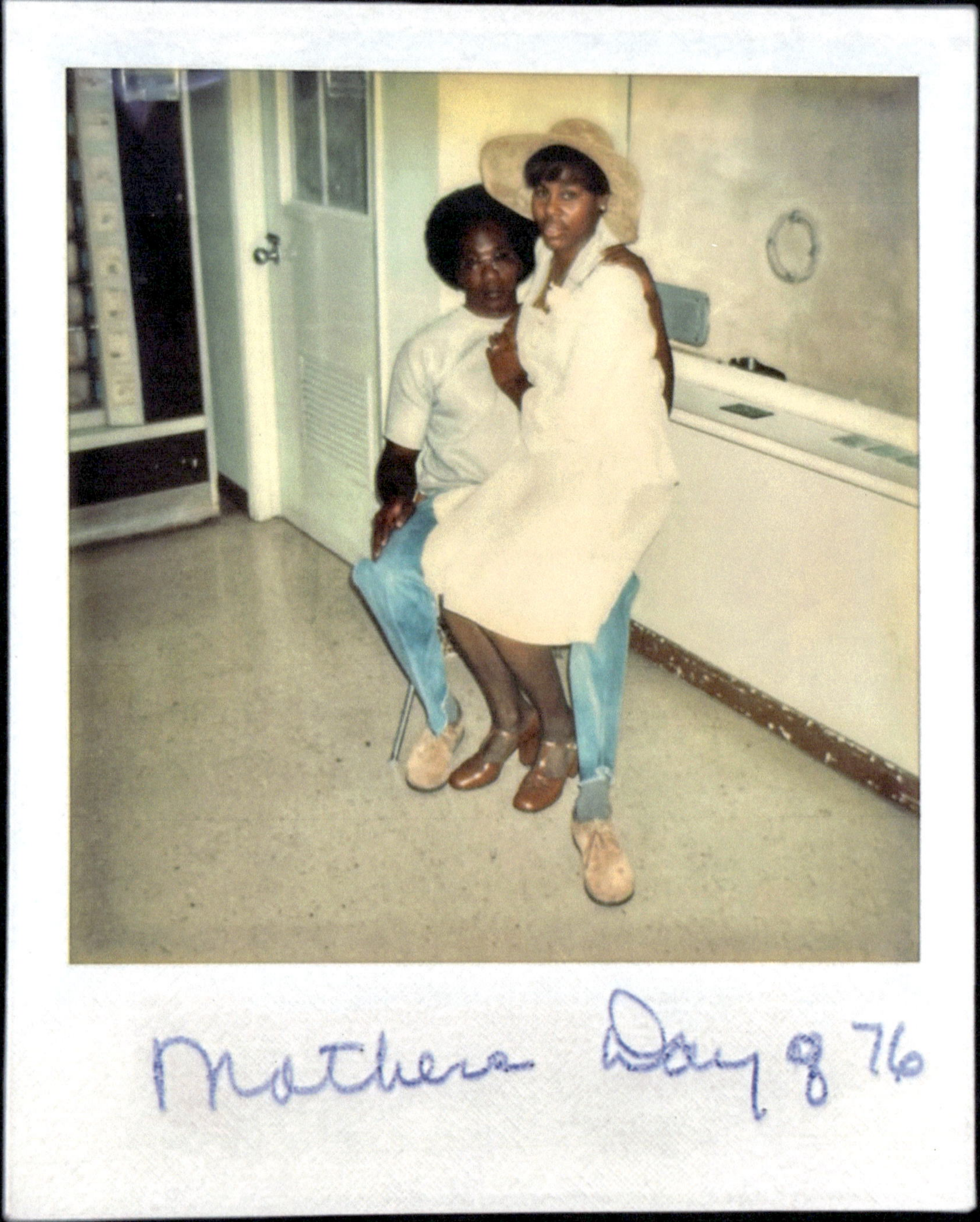

This picture was taken in the visiting area of Tehachapi State Prison on May 9, 1976

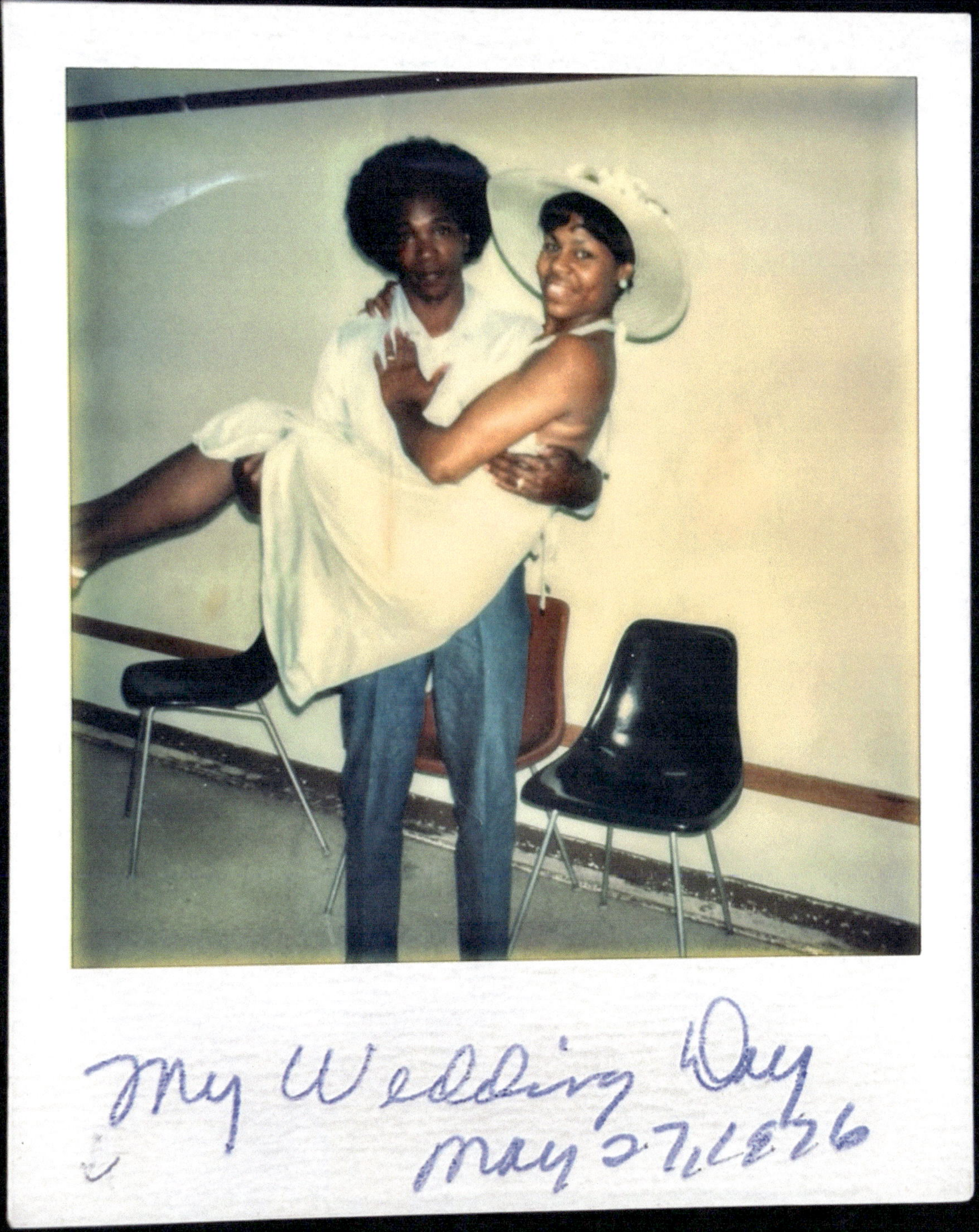

This picture was taken in the visiting area of Tehachapi State Prison on May 27, 1976

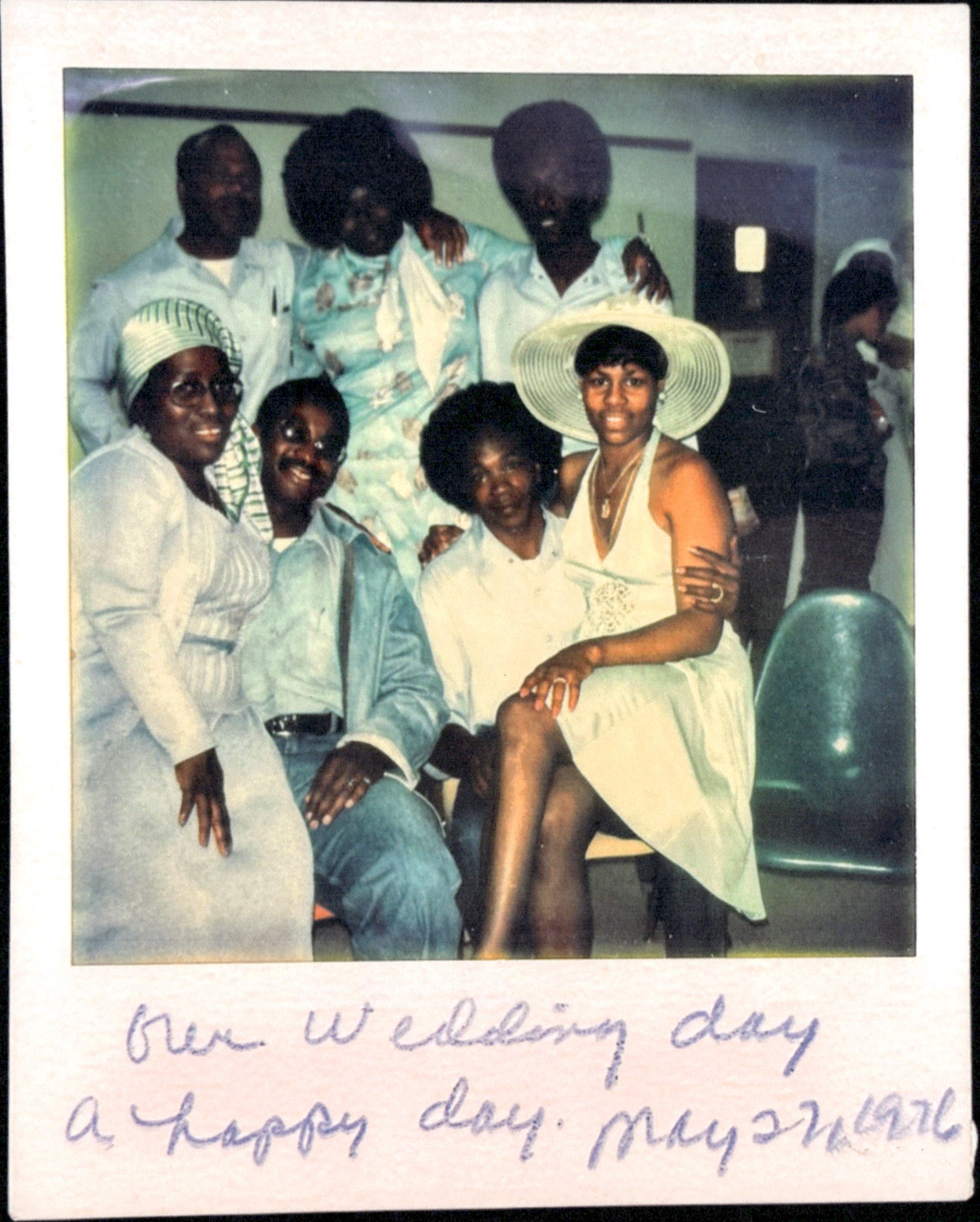

This picture was taken in the visiting area of Tehachapi State Prison on May 27, 1976.

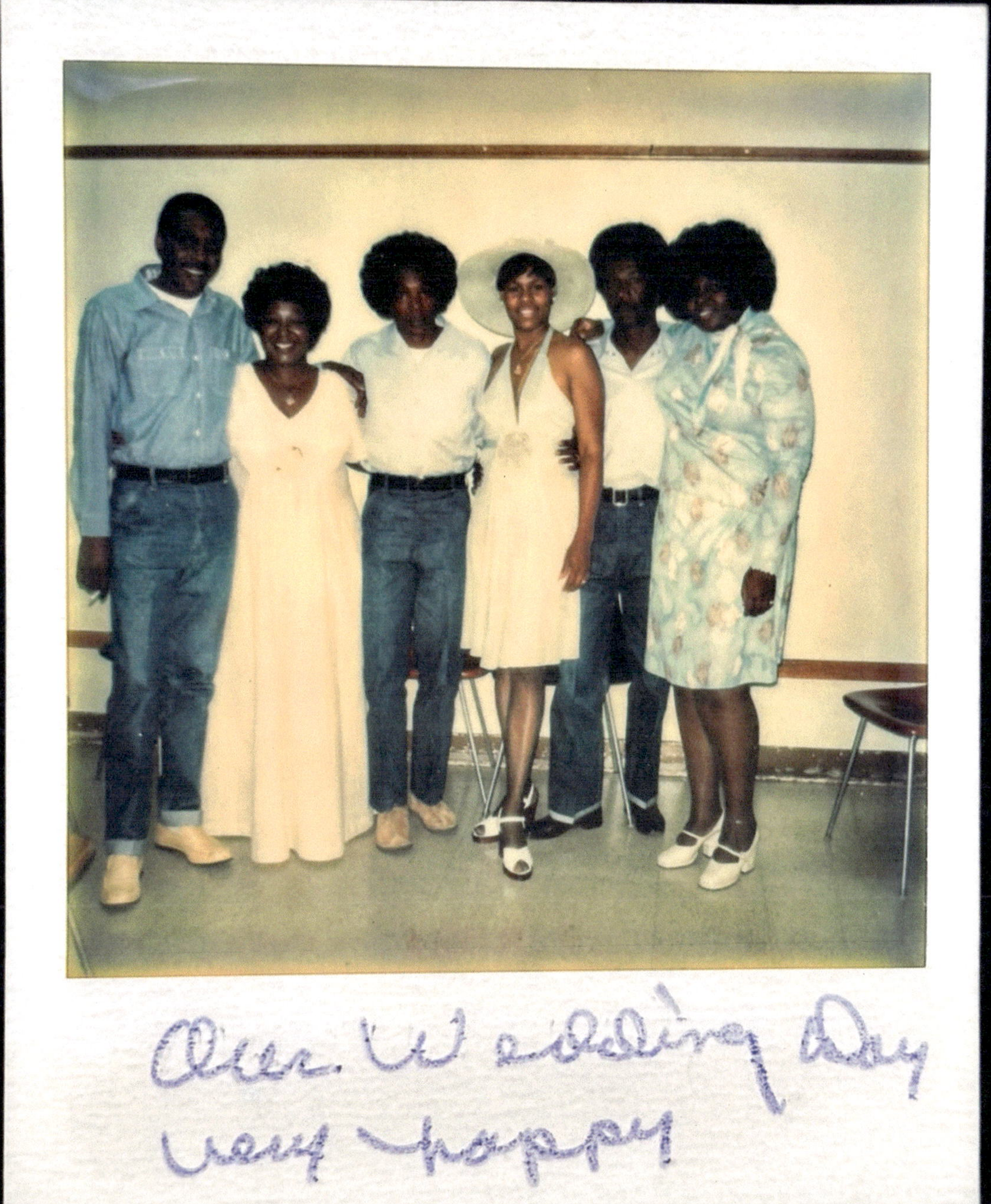

This picture was taken in the visiting area of Tehachapi State Prison on May 27, 1976.

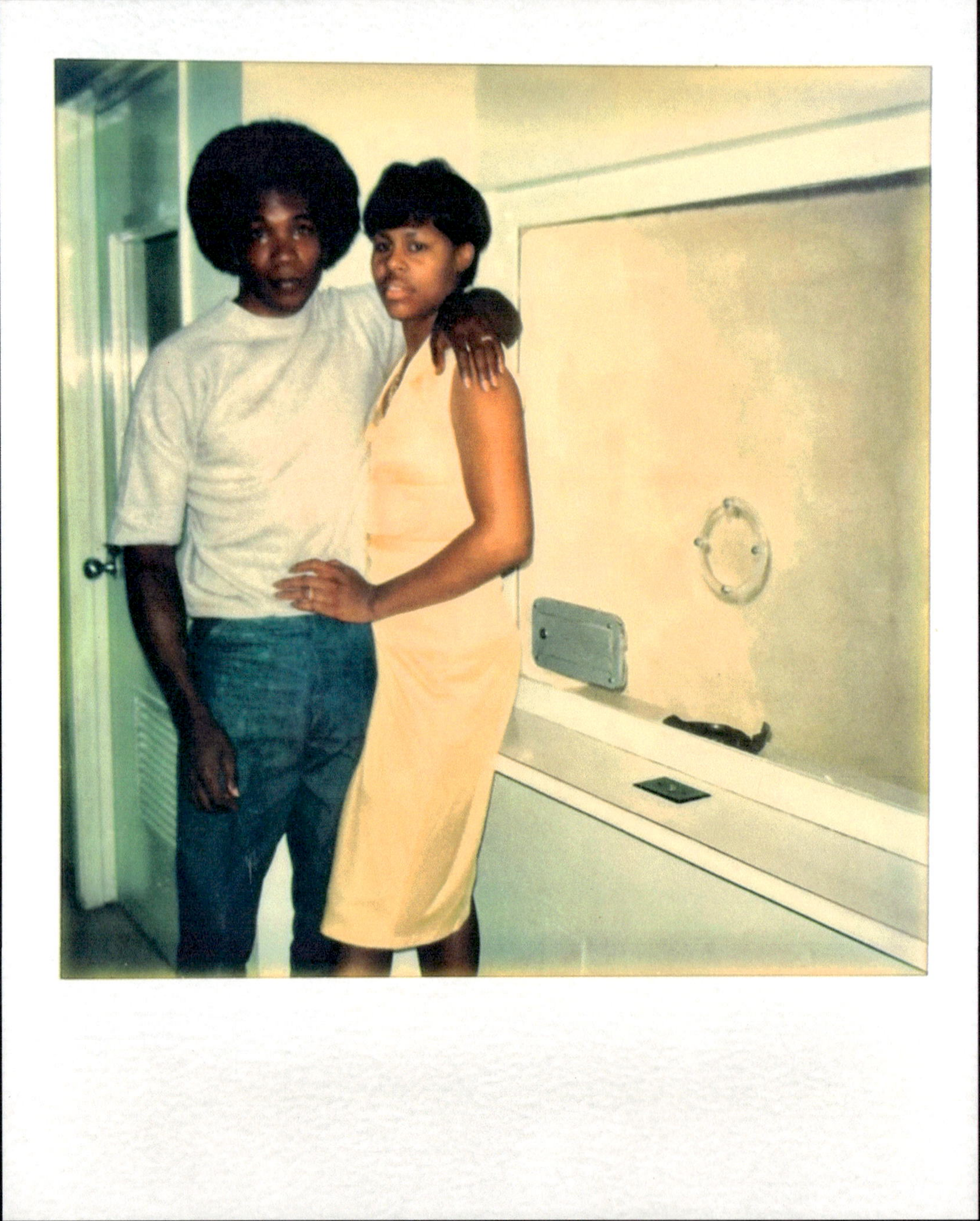

his picture was taken in the visiting area of Tehachapi State Prison on May 29, 1976

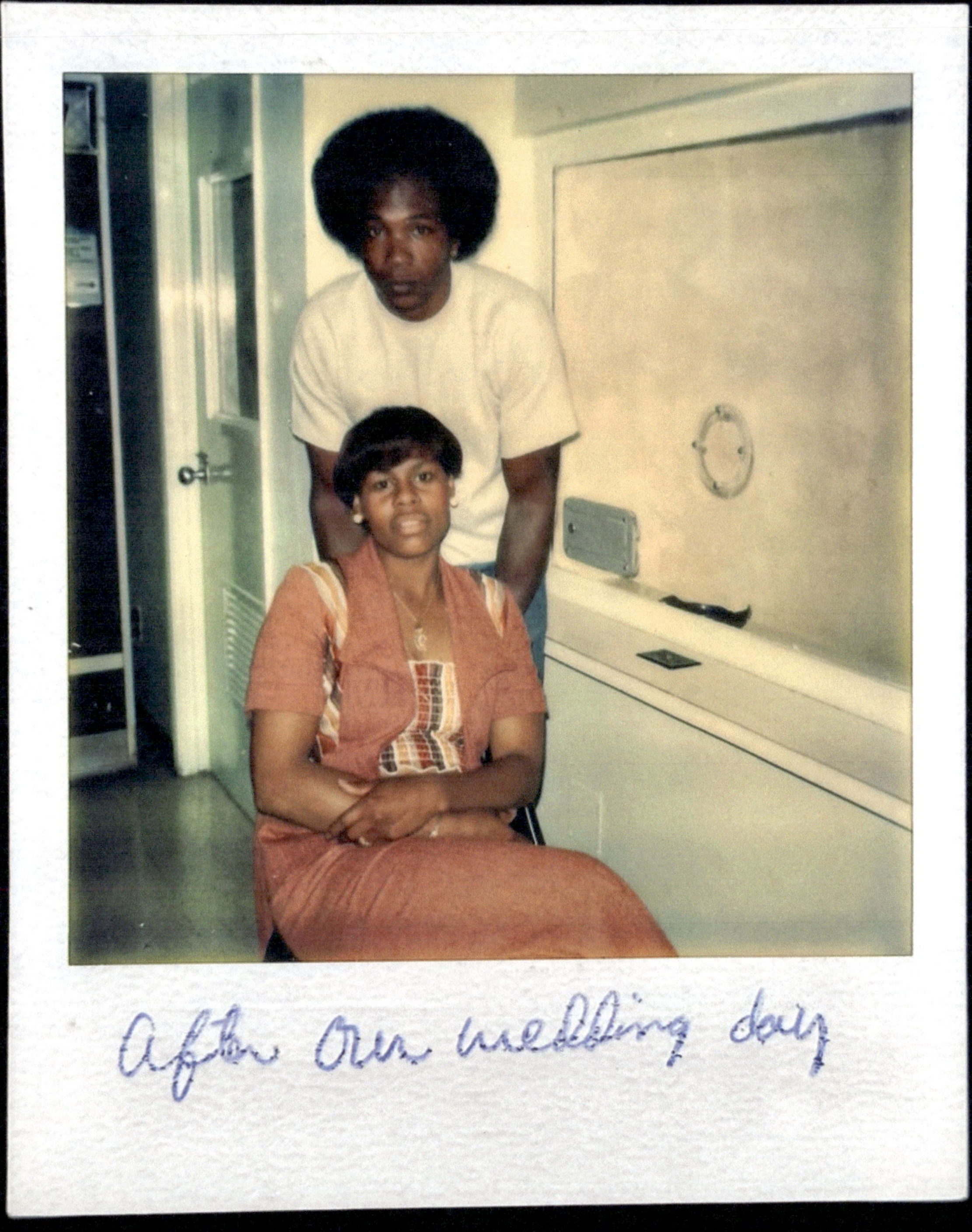

This picture was taken in the visiting area of Tehachapi State Prison on May 30, 1976

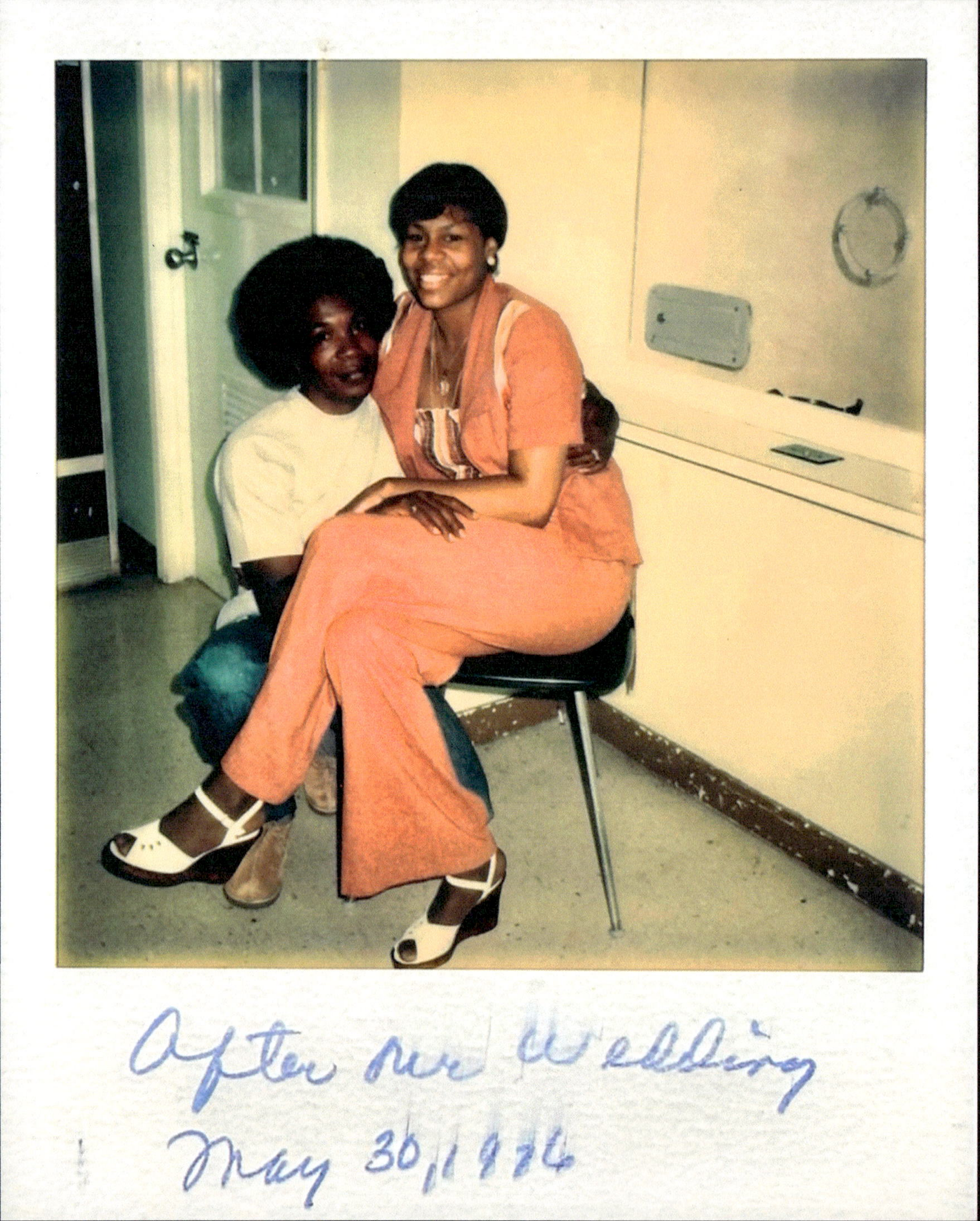

is picture was taken in the visiting area of Tehachapi State Prison on May 30, 1976.

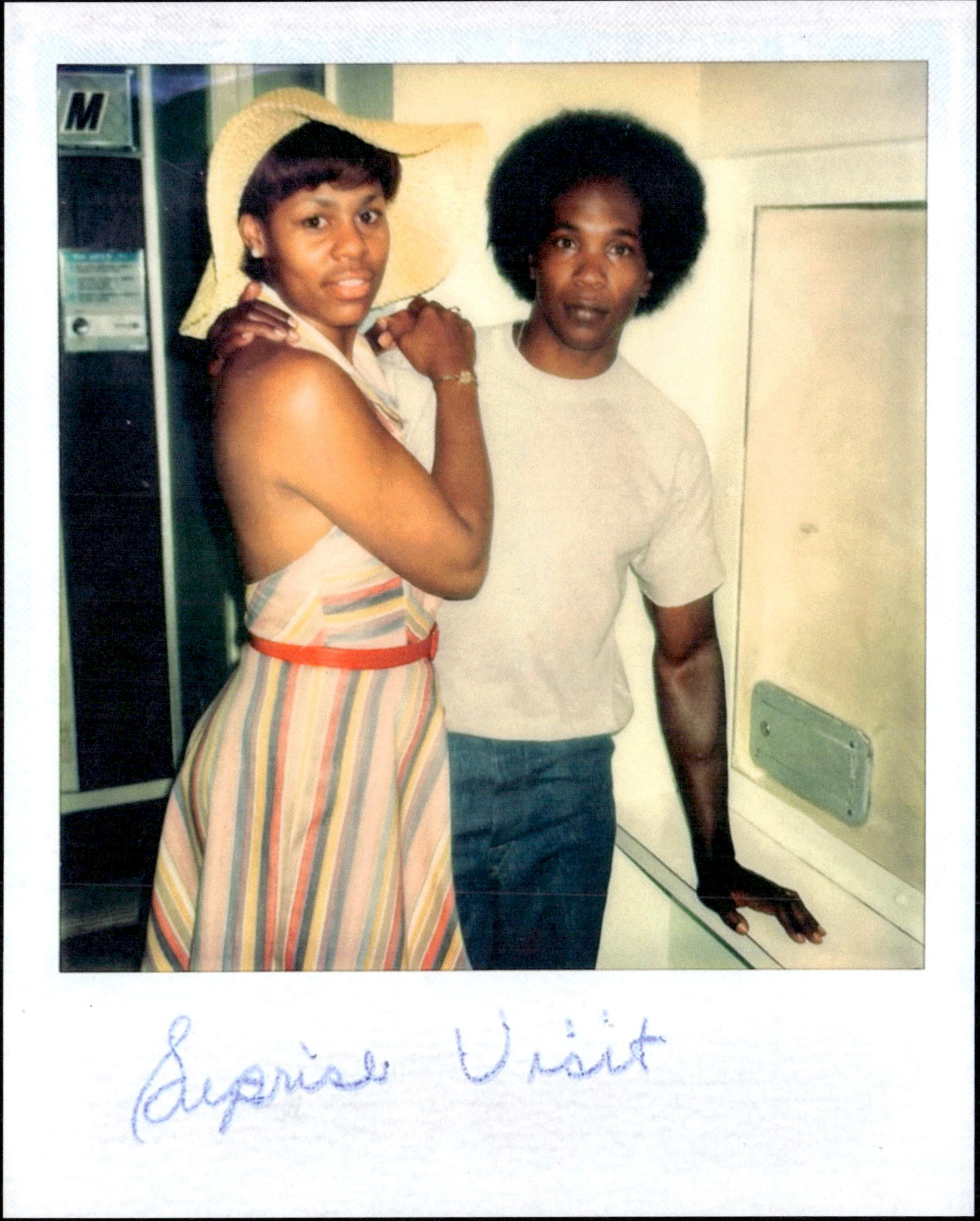

This picture was taken in the visiting area of Tehachapi State Prison on June 19, 1976.

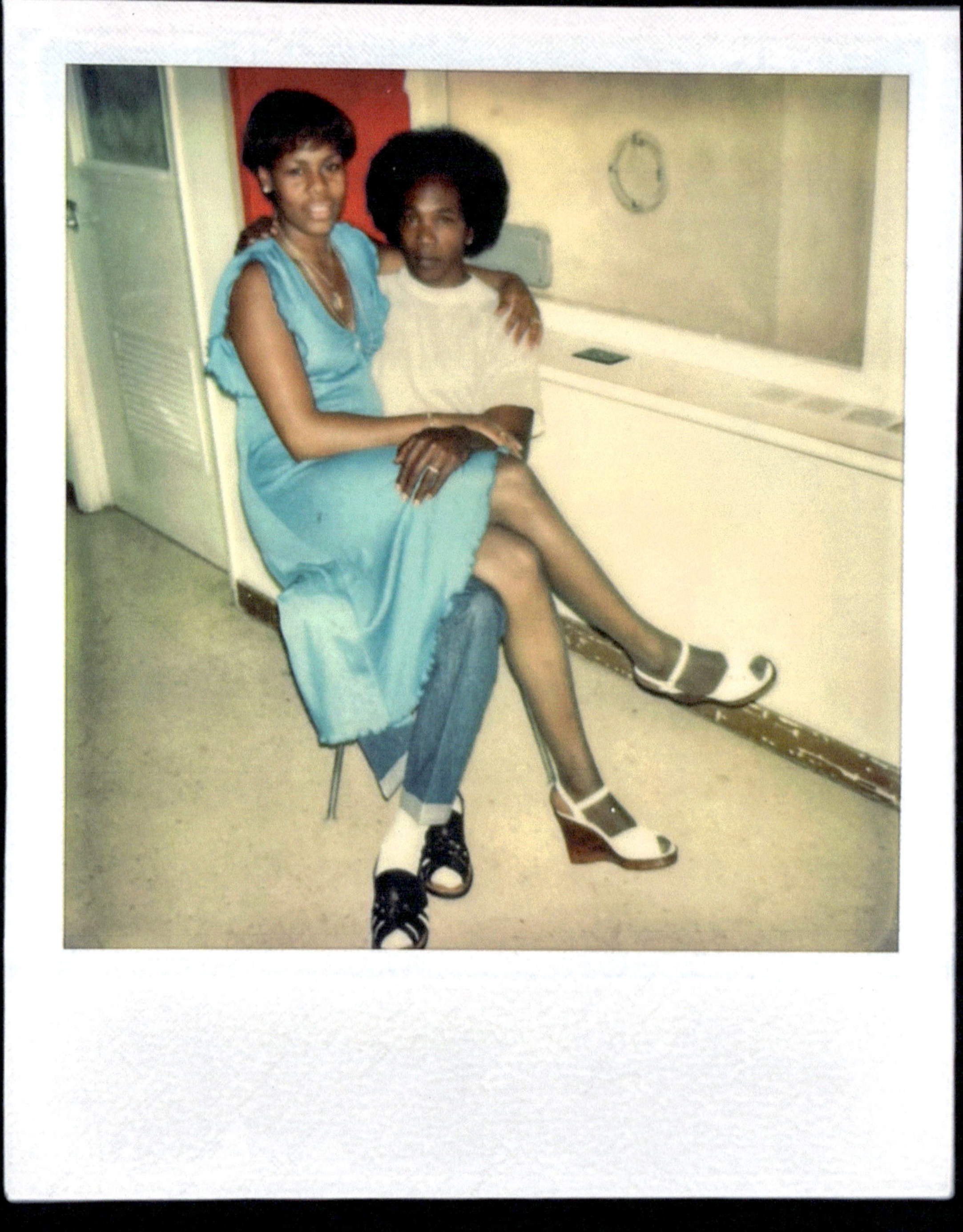

This picture was taken in the visiting area of Tehachapi State Prison on July 25, 1976.

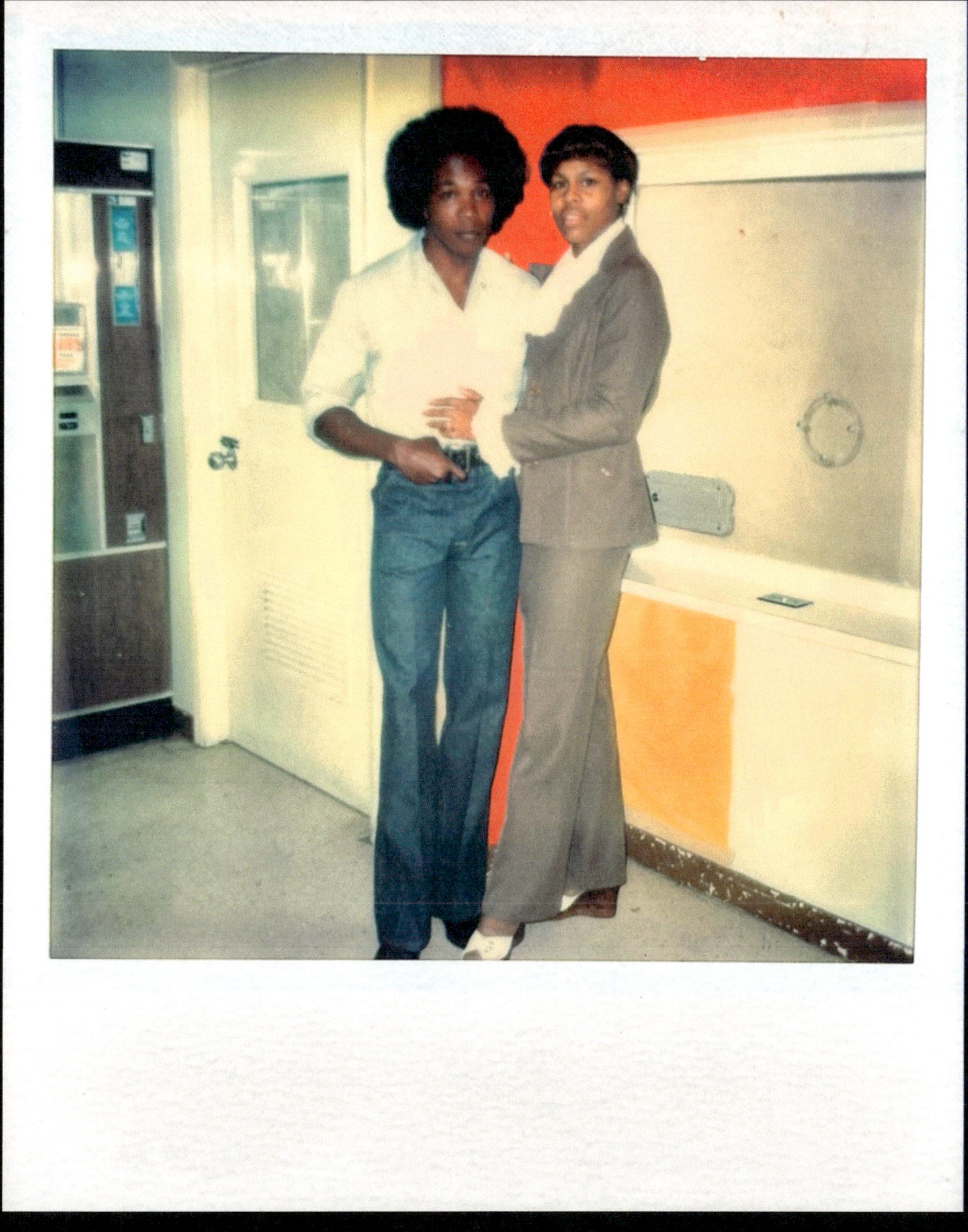

This picture was taken in the visiting area of Tehachapi State Prison on October 30, 1976

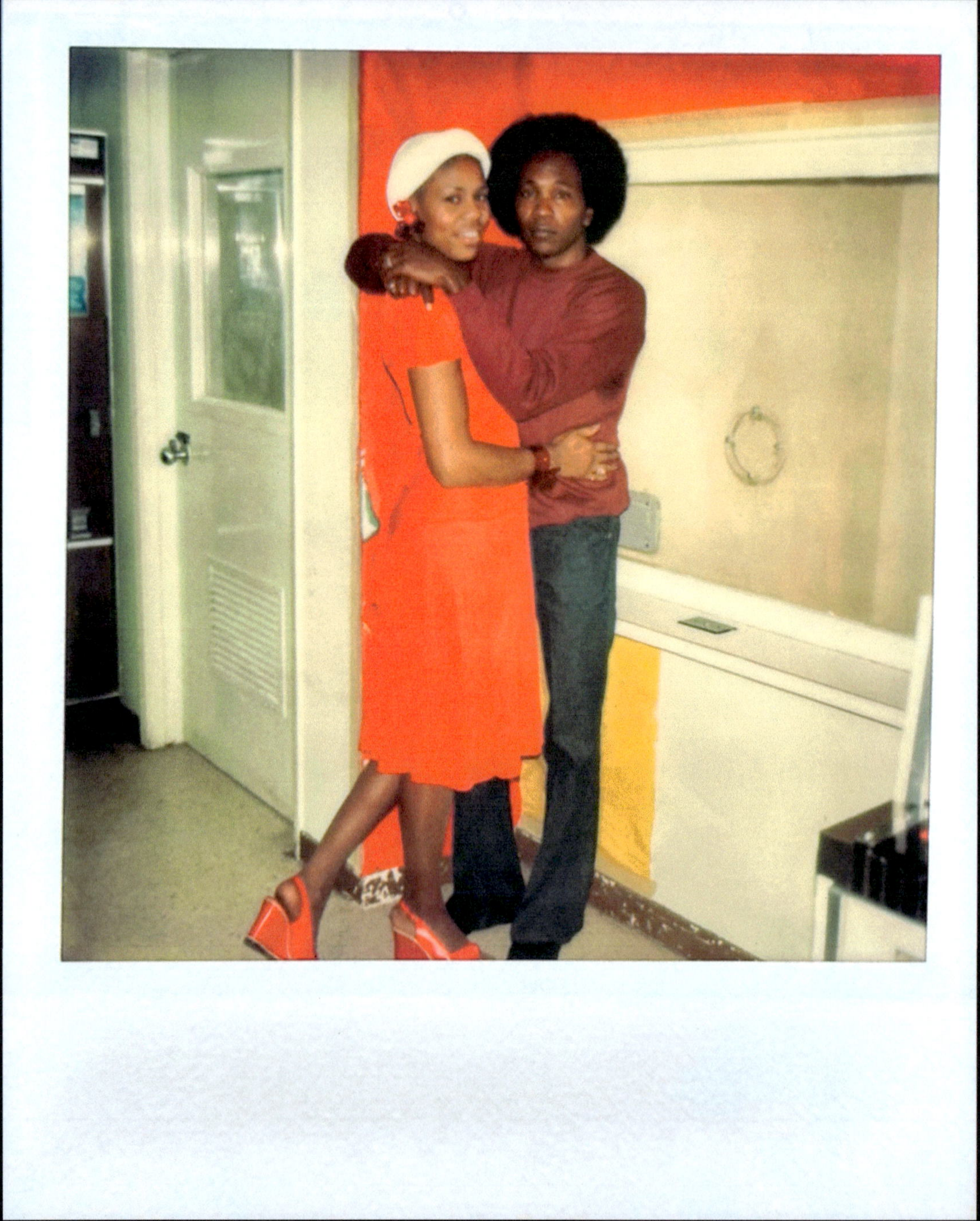

This picture was taken in the visiting area of Tehachapi State Prison on October 31, 1976

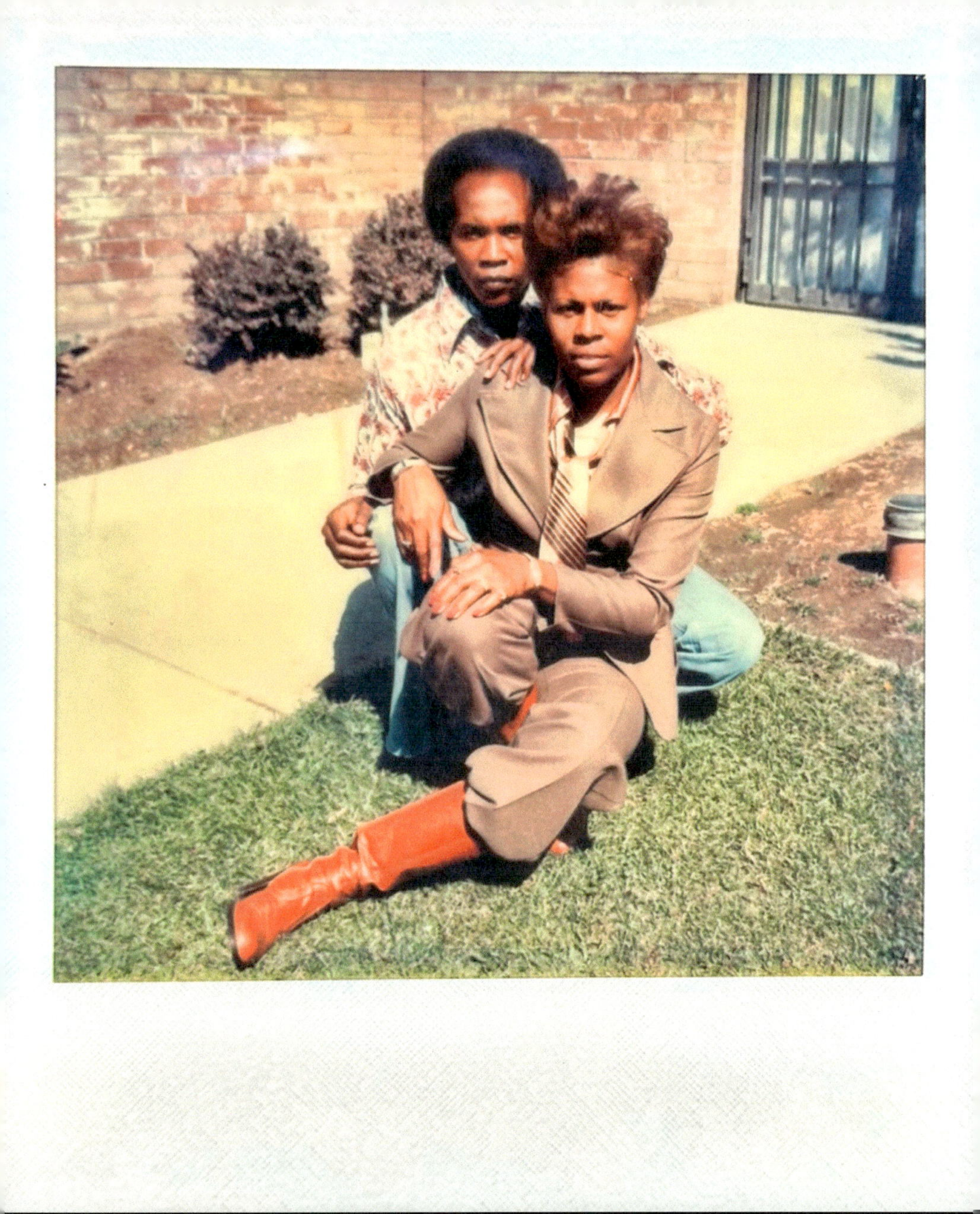

This picture was taken in the visiting area of Tehachapi State Prison

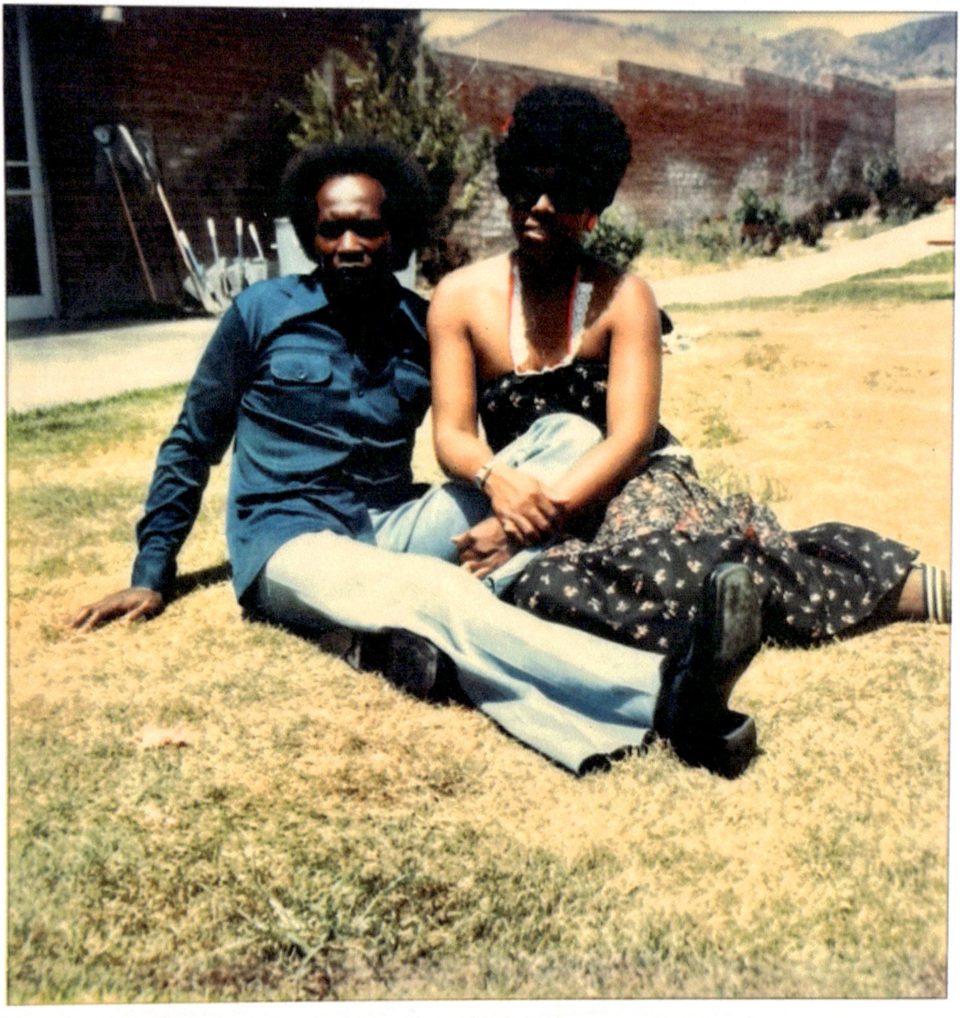

This picture was taken in the visiting area of Tehachapi State Prison

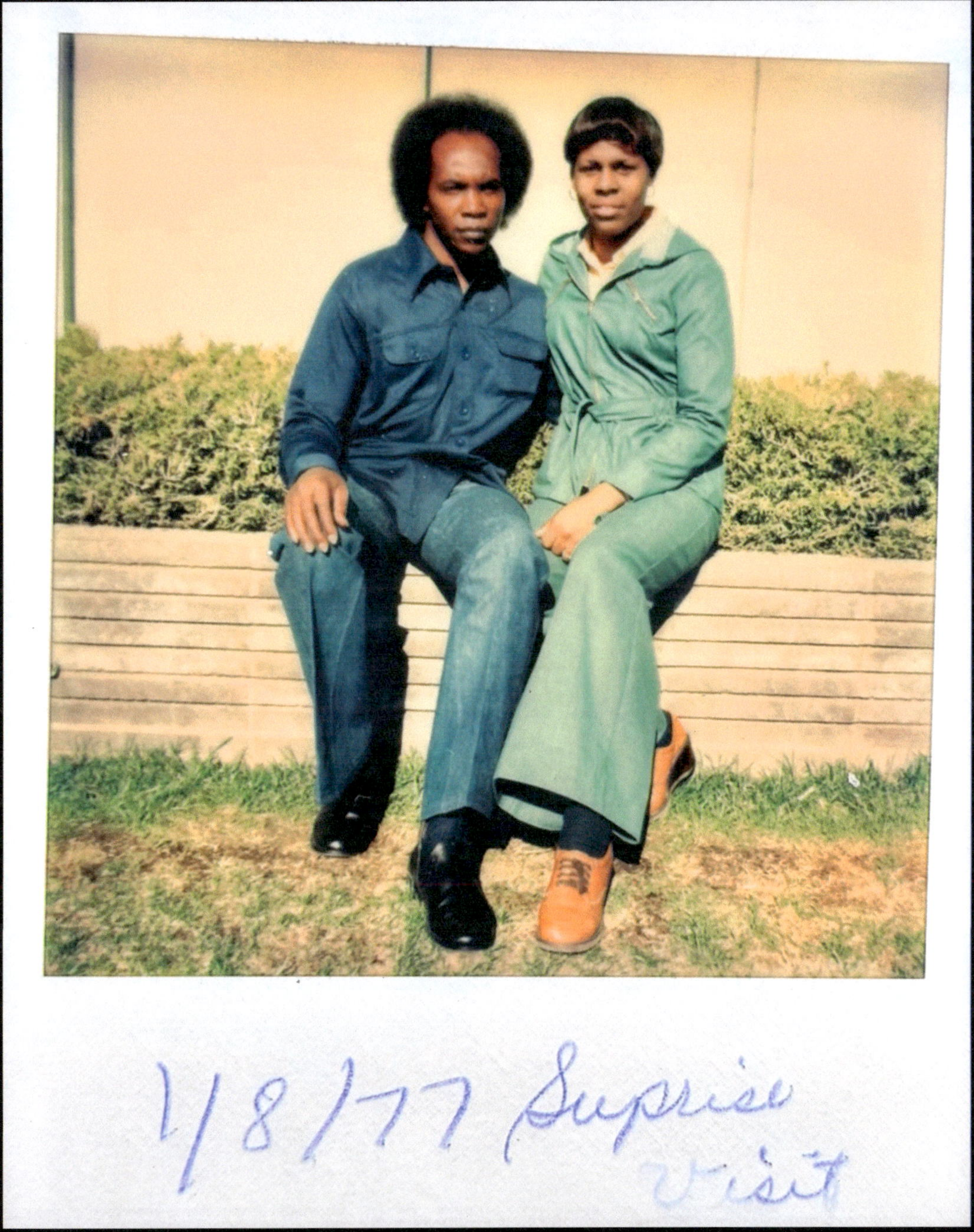

This picture was taken in the visiting area of California Men's Colony State Prison on January 8, 1977.

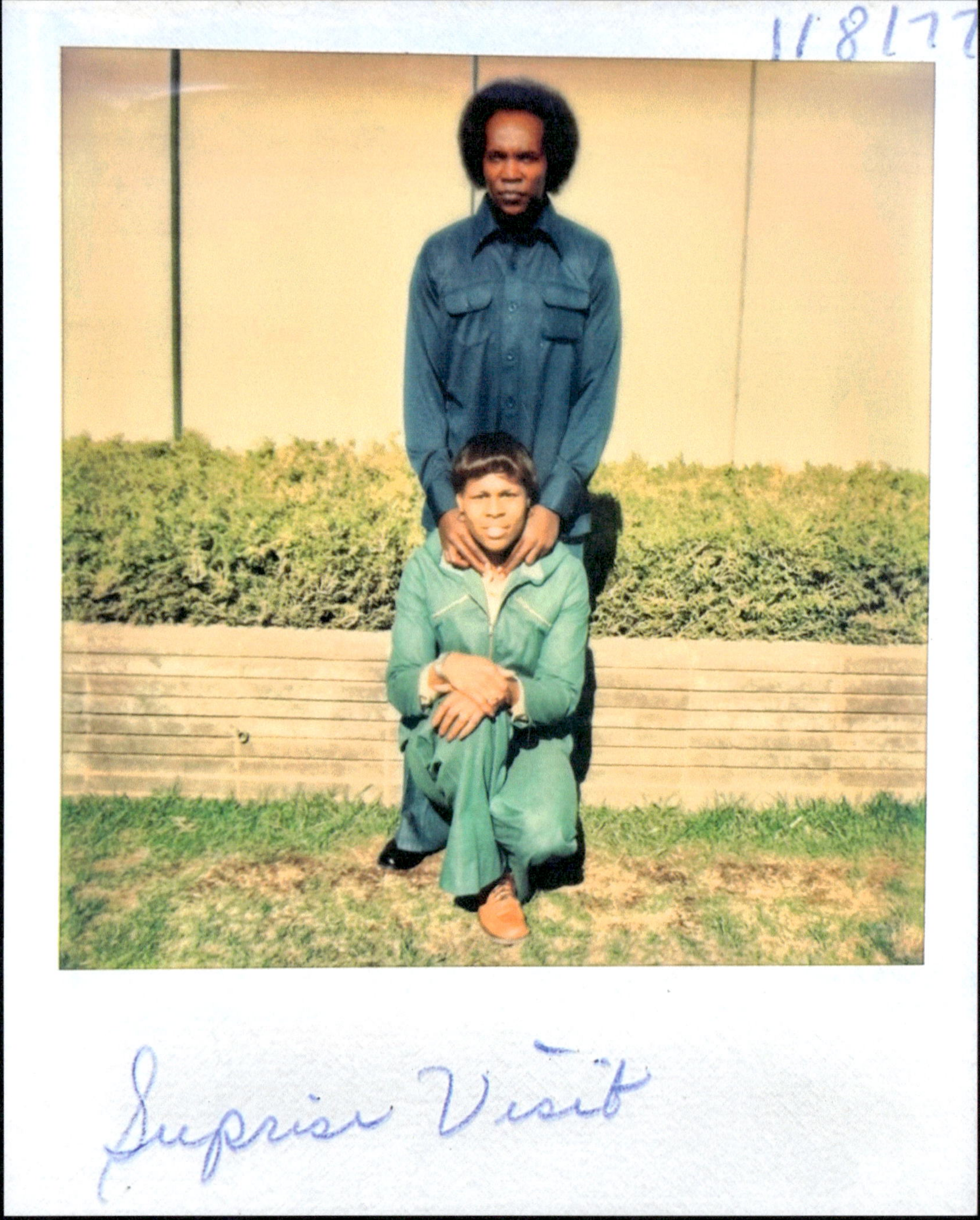

This picture was taken in the visiting area of California Men's Colony State Prison on January 8, 1977.

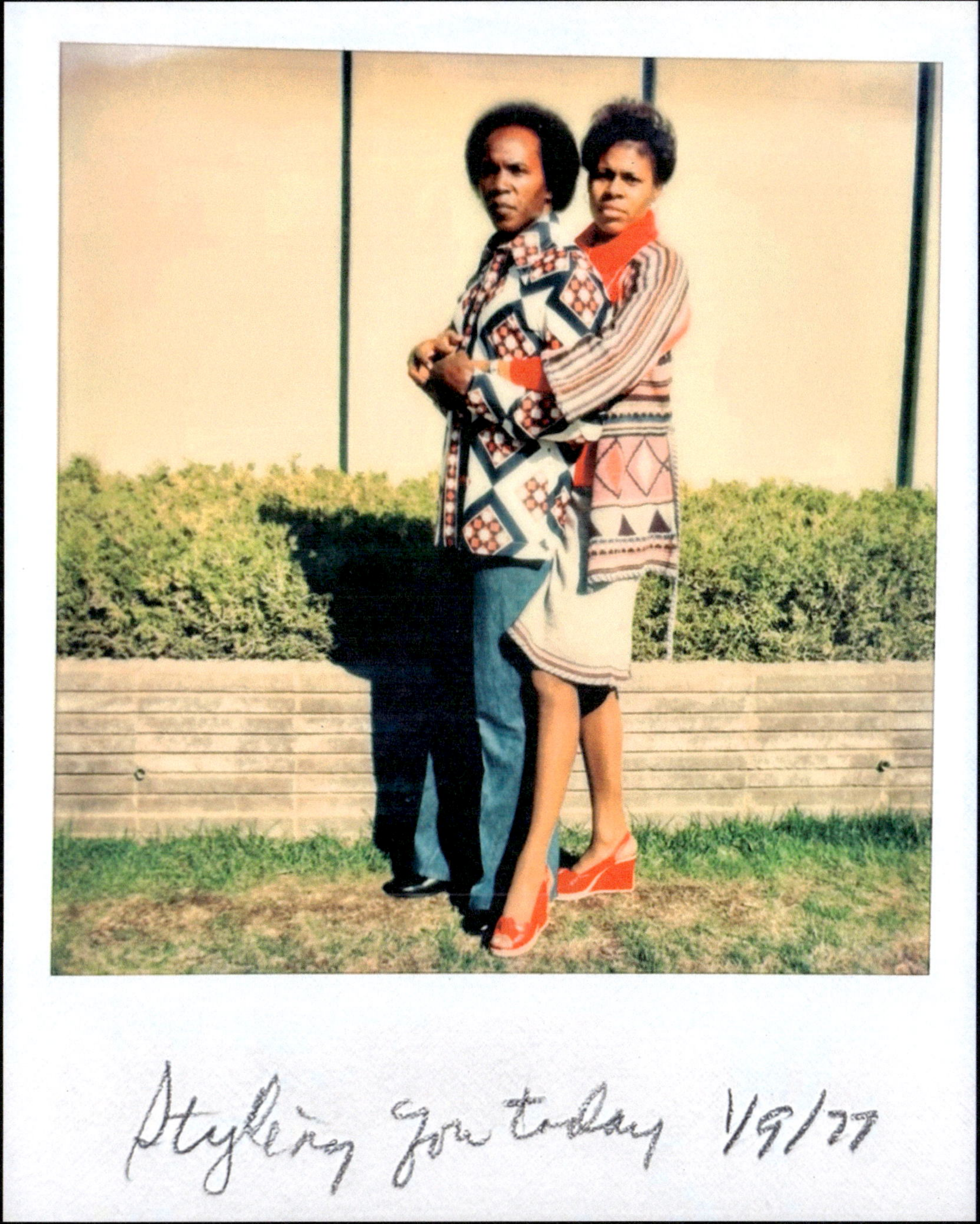

This picture was taken in the visiting area of Càlifornia Men's Colony State Prison on January 9, 1977.

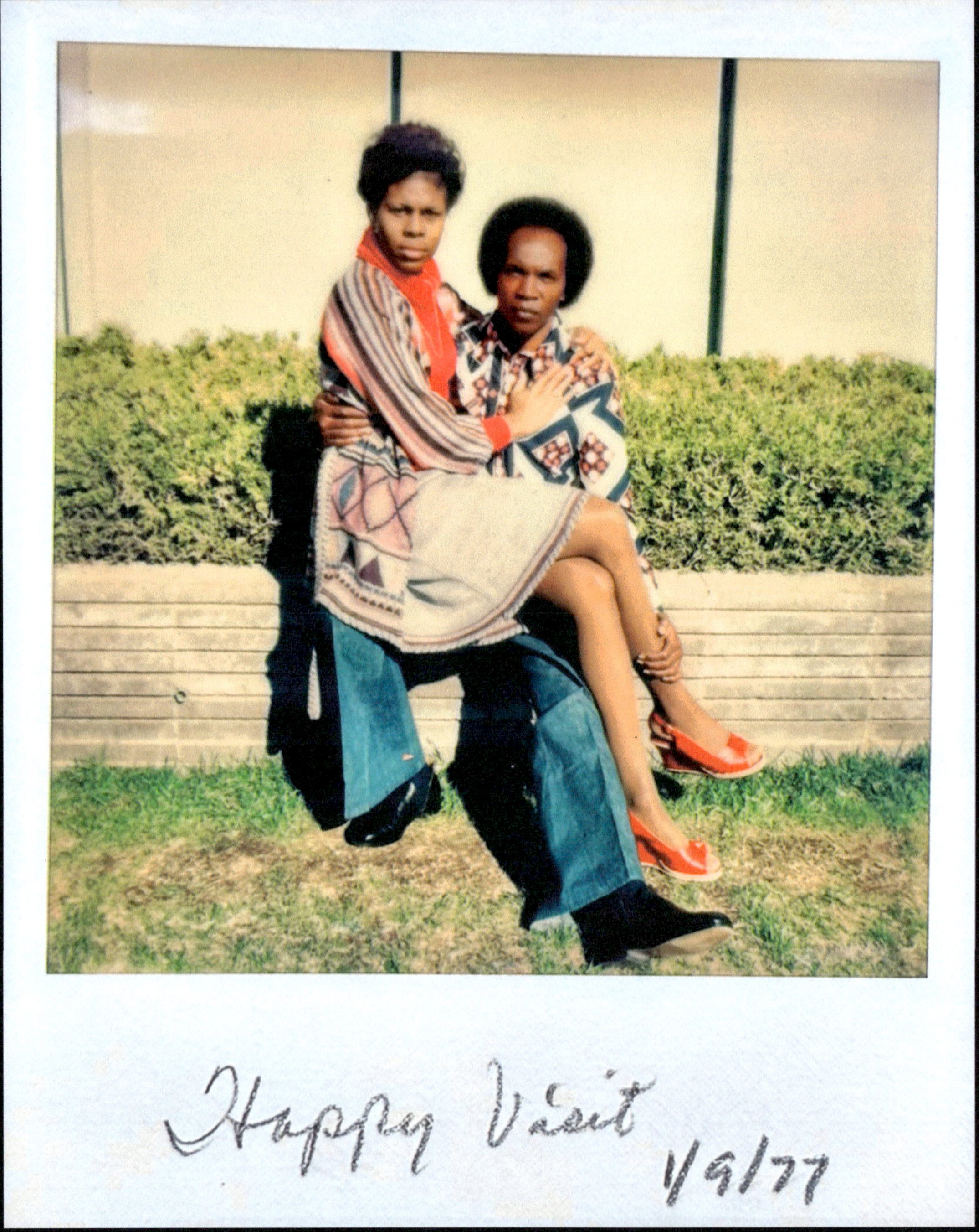

This picture was taken in the visiting area of California Men's Colony State Prison on January 9, 1977.

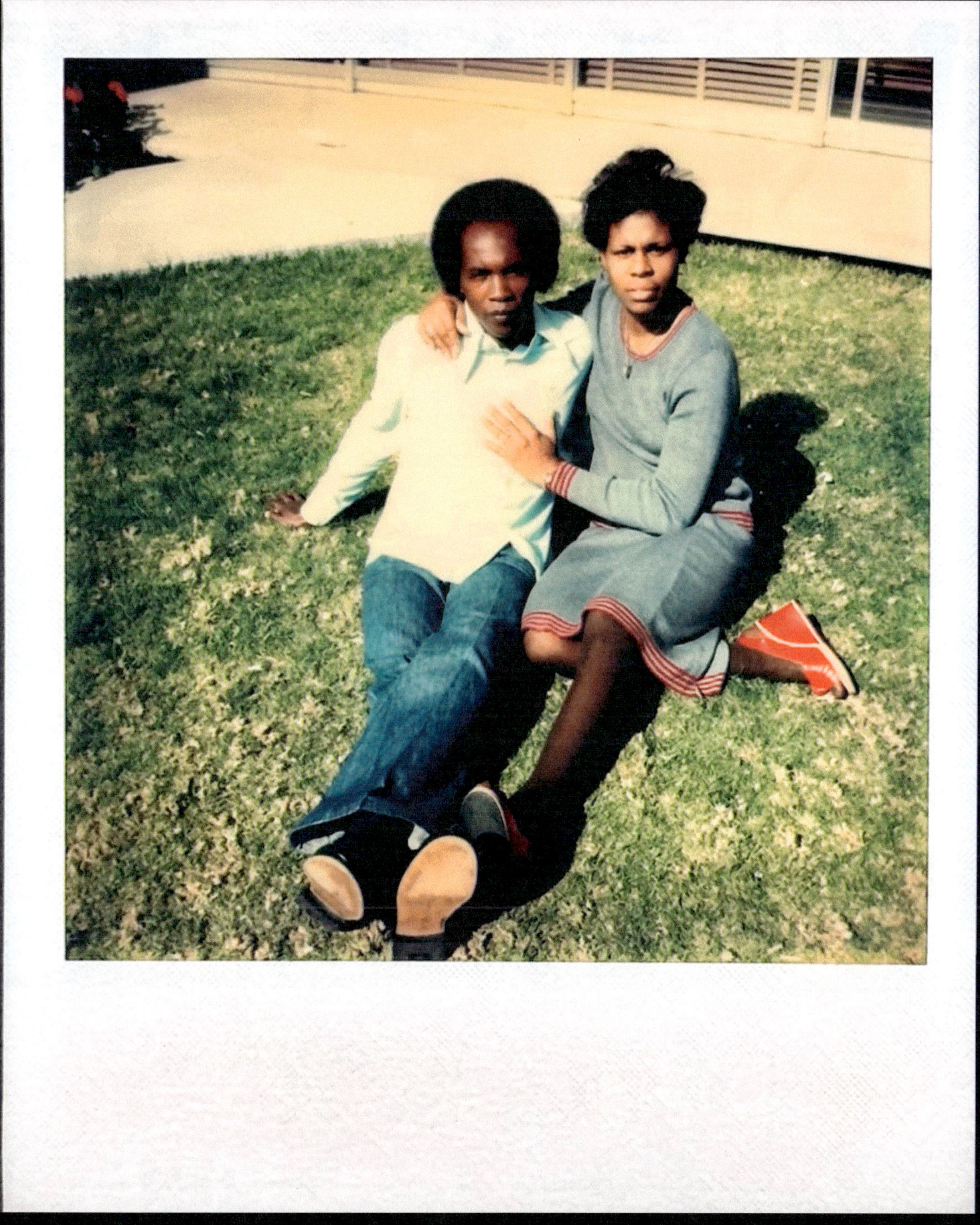

his picture was taken in the visiting area of California Men's Colony State Prison on
February 5, 1977.

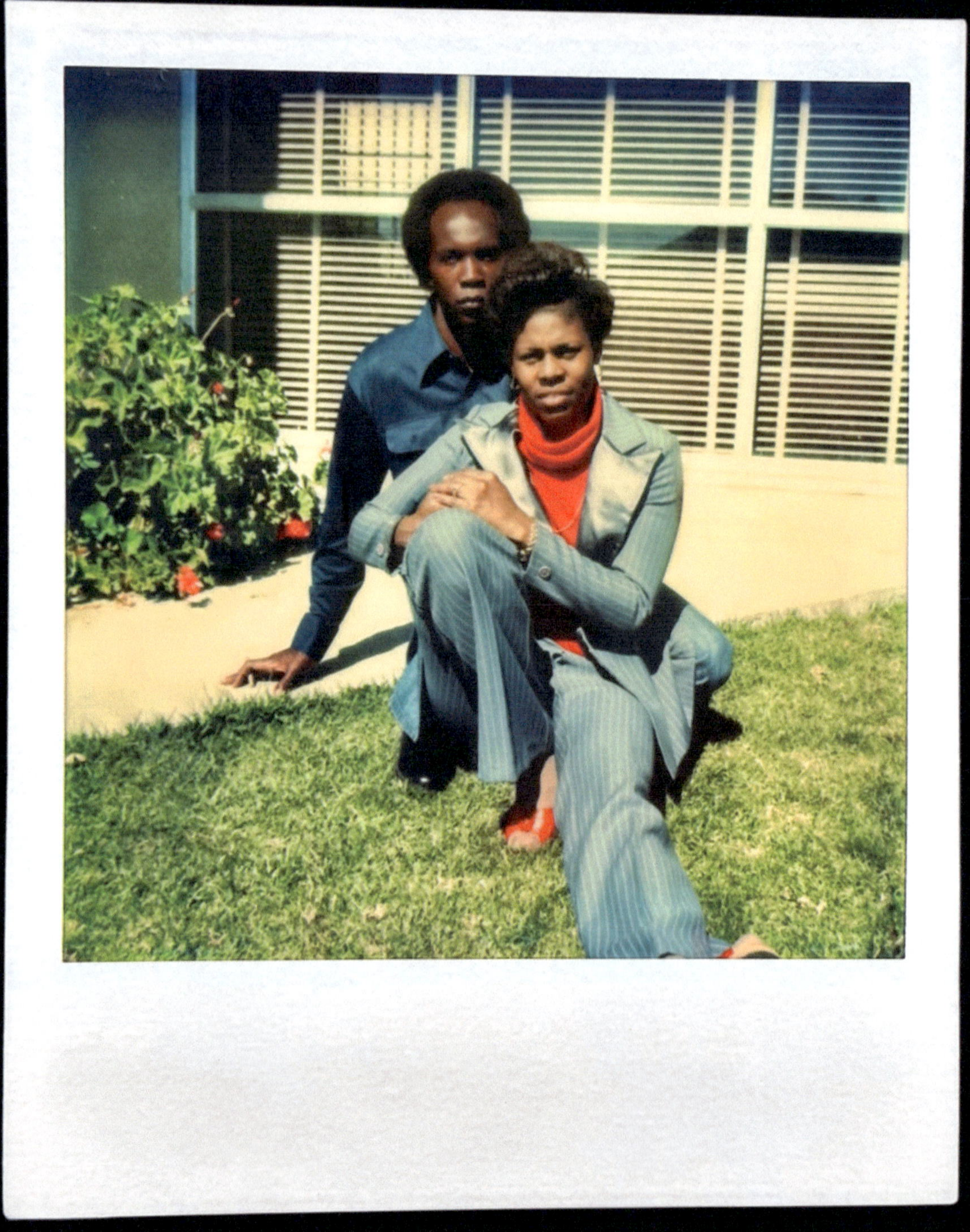

his picture was taken in the visiting area of California Men's Colony State Prison on
February 27, 1977.

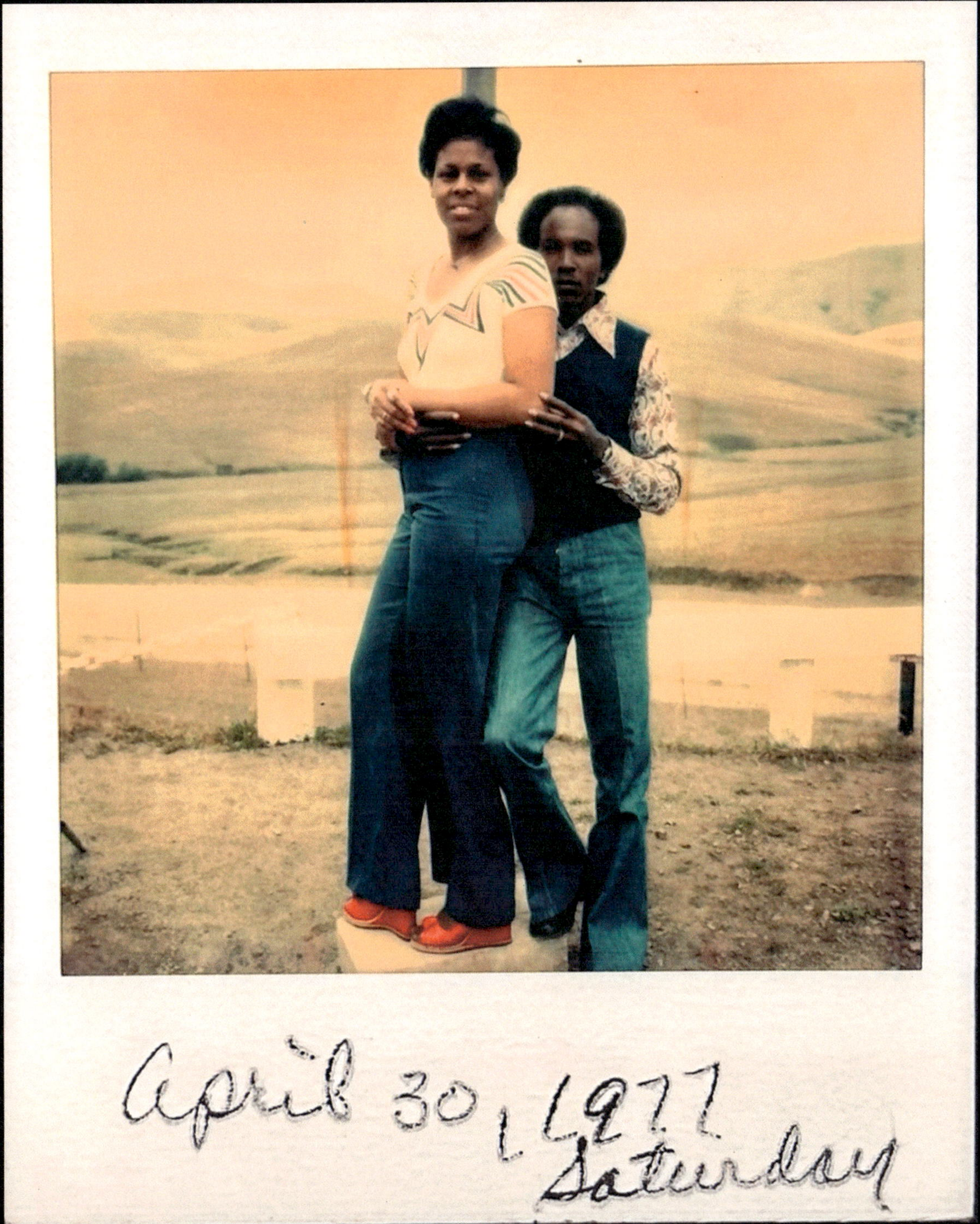

s picture was taken in the visiting area of California Men's Colony State Prison on April 30, 1977.

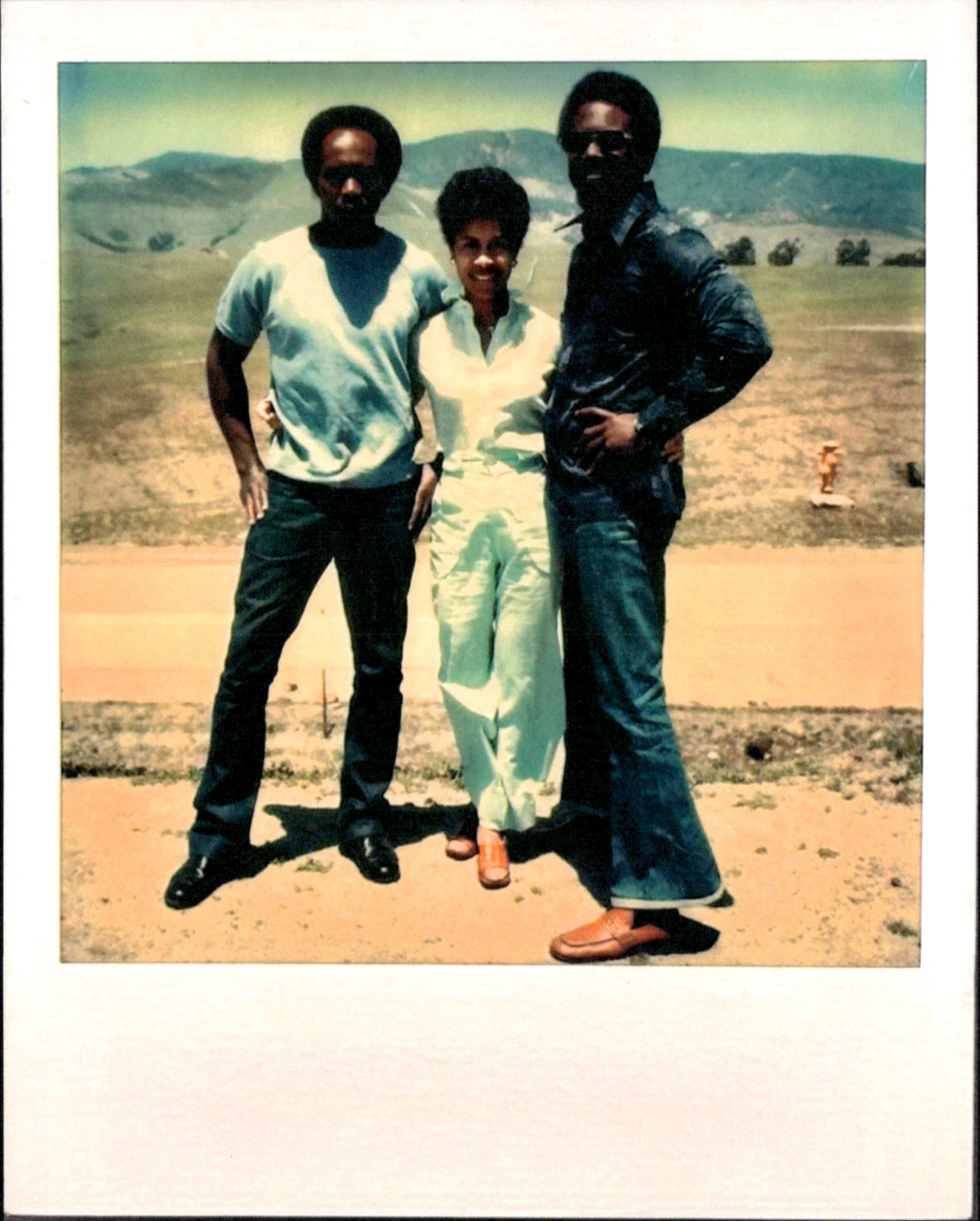

This picture was taken in the visiting area of California Men's Colony State Prison on May 22, 1977.

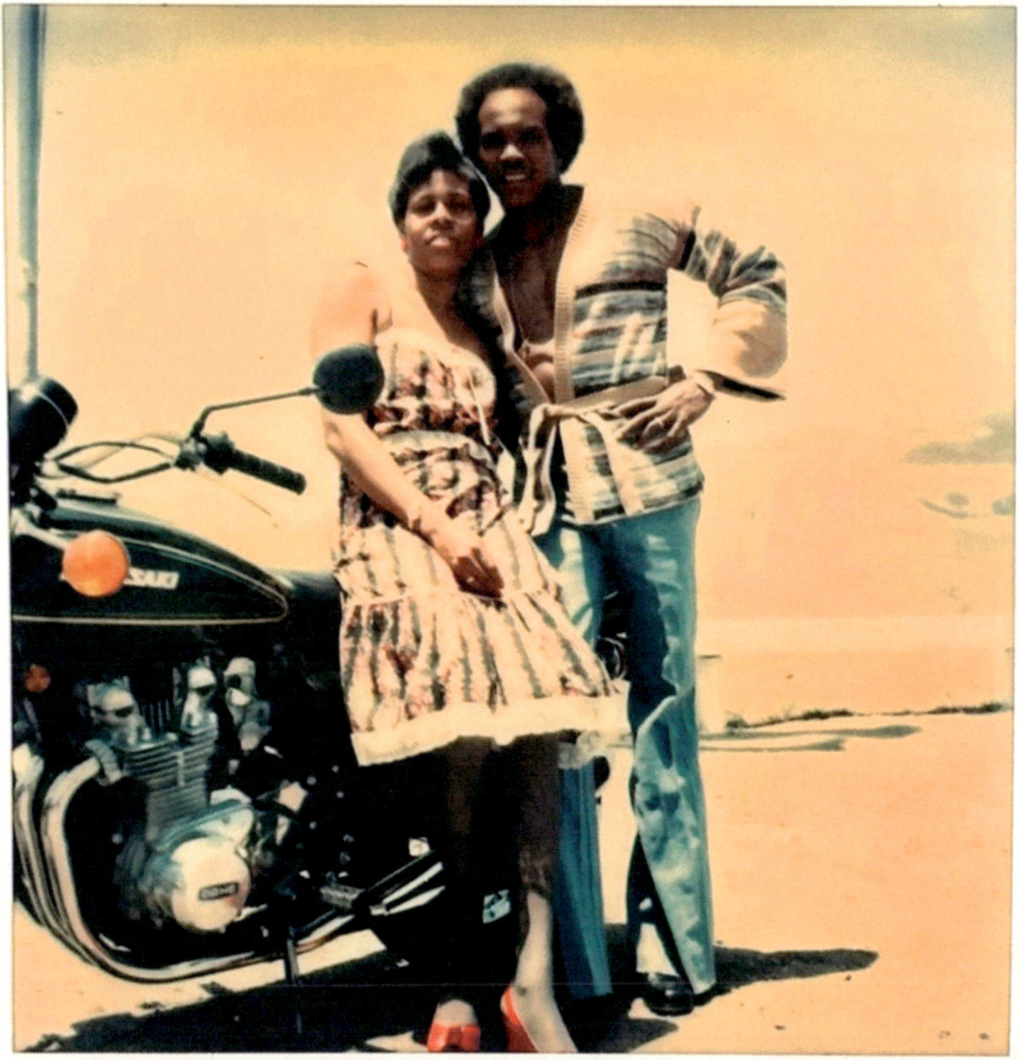

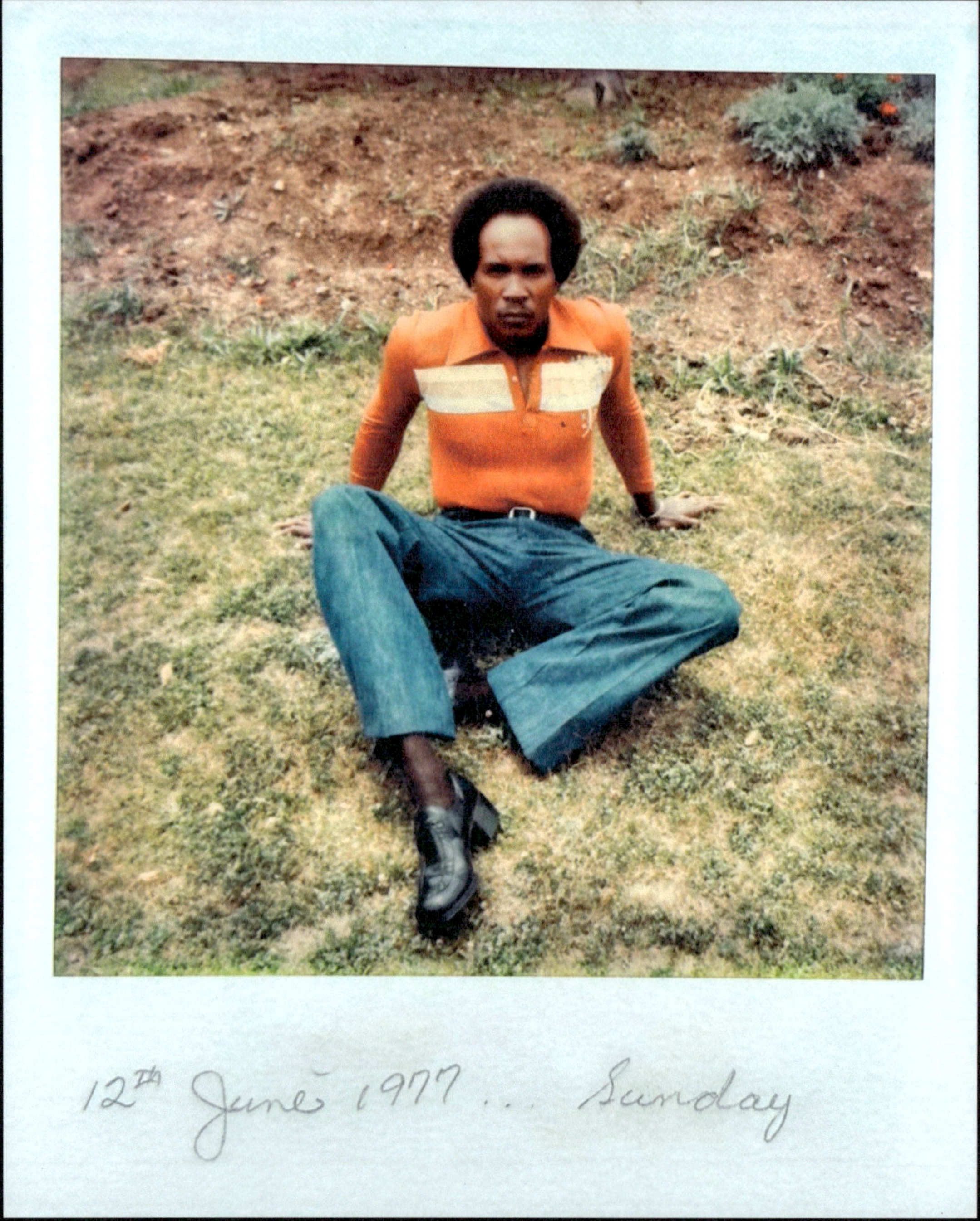

This picture was taken in the visiting area of California Men's Colony State Prison on June 12, 1977.

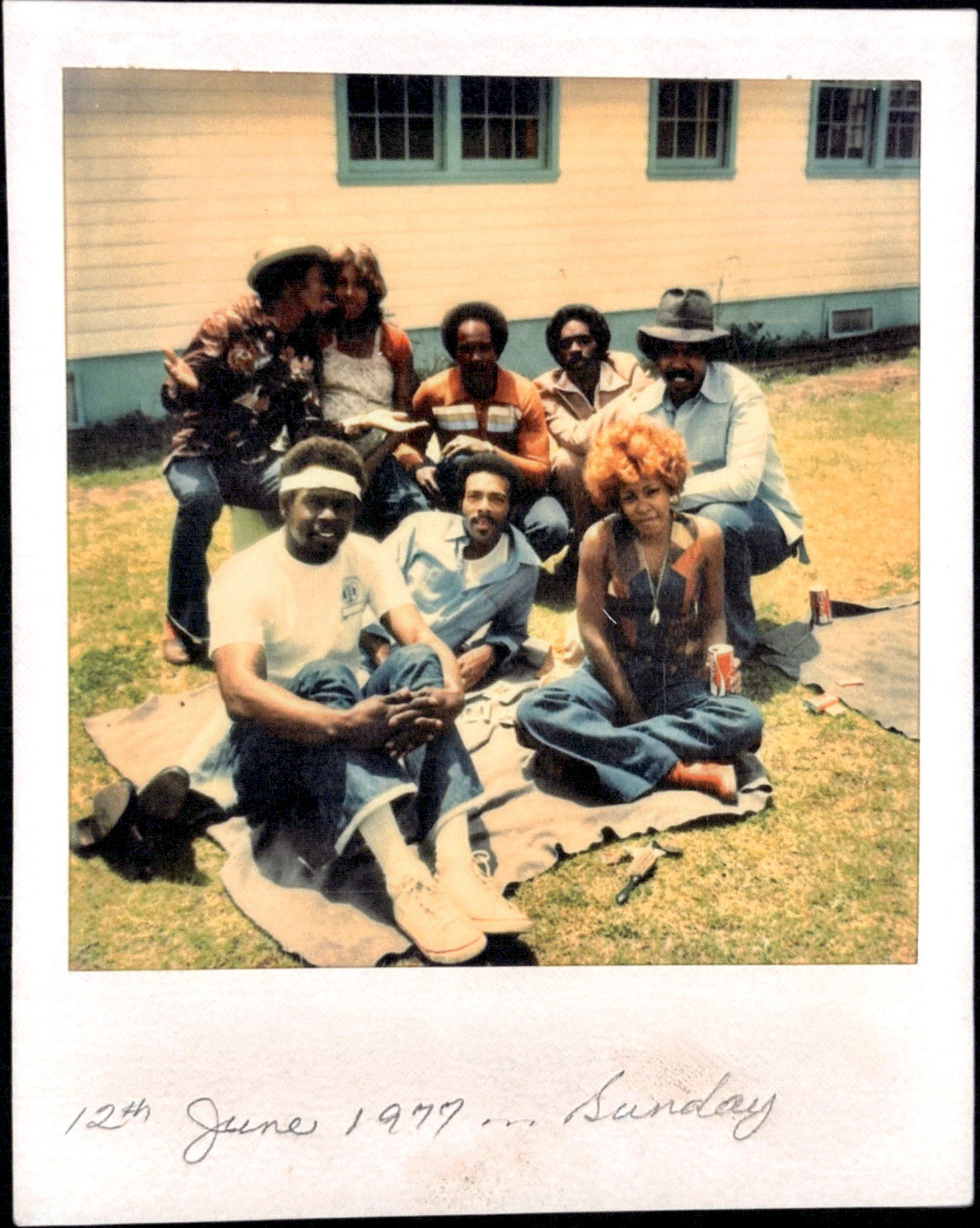

This picture was taken in the visiting area of California Men's Colony State Prison on 12, 1977.

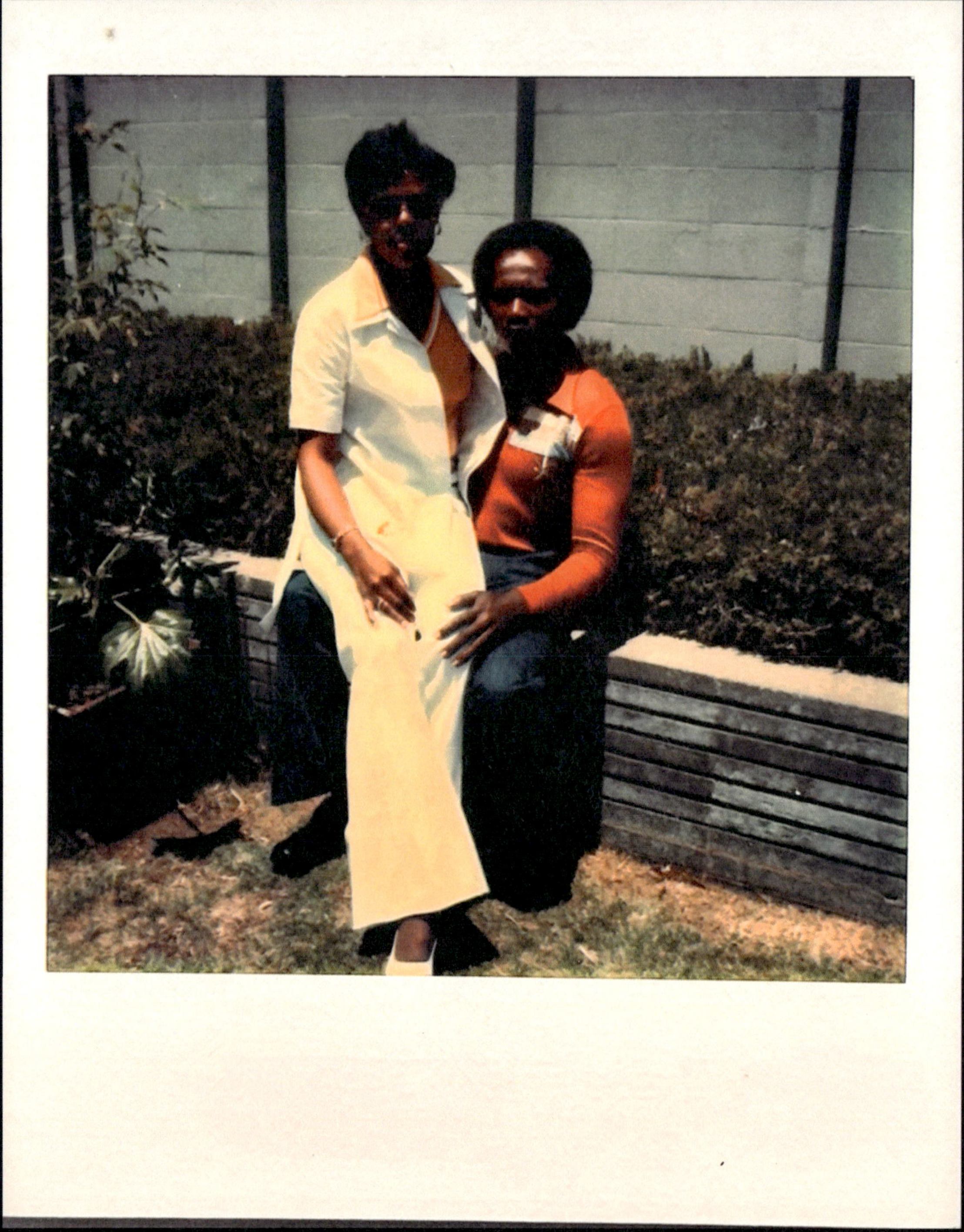

This picture was taken in the visiting area of California Men's Colony State Prison on June 25, 1977.

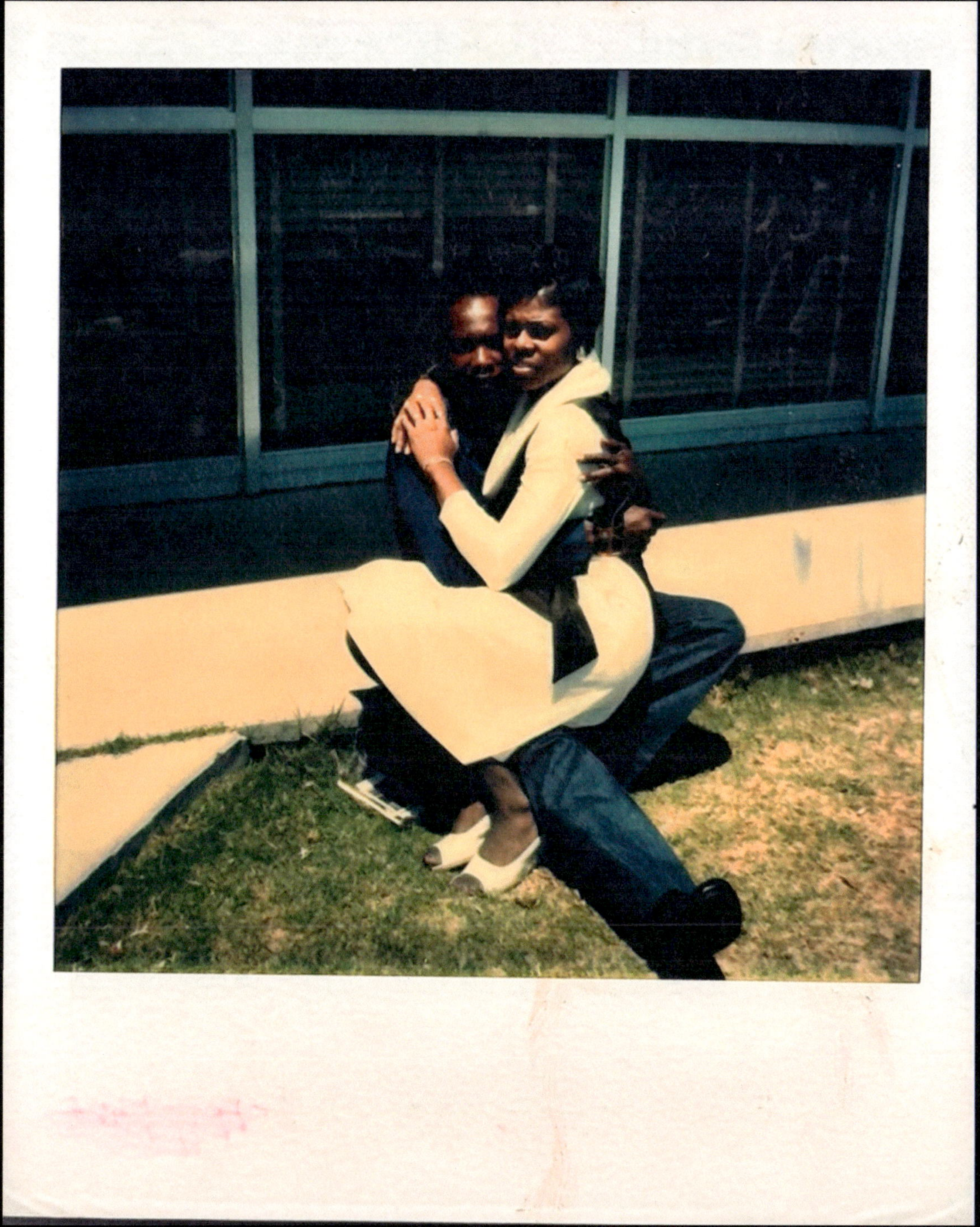

This picture was taken in the visiting area of California Men's Colony State Prison on June 26, 1977.

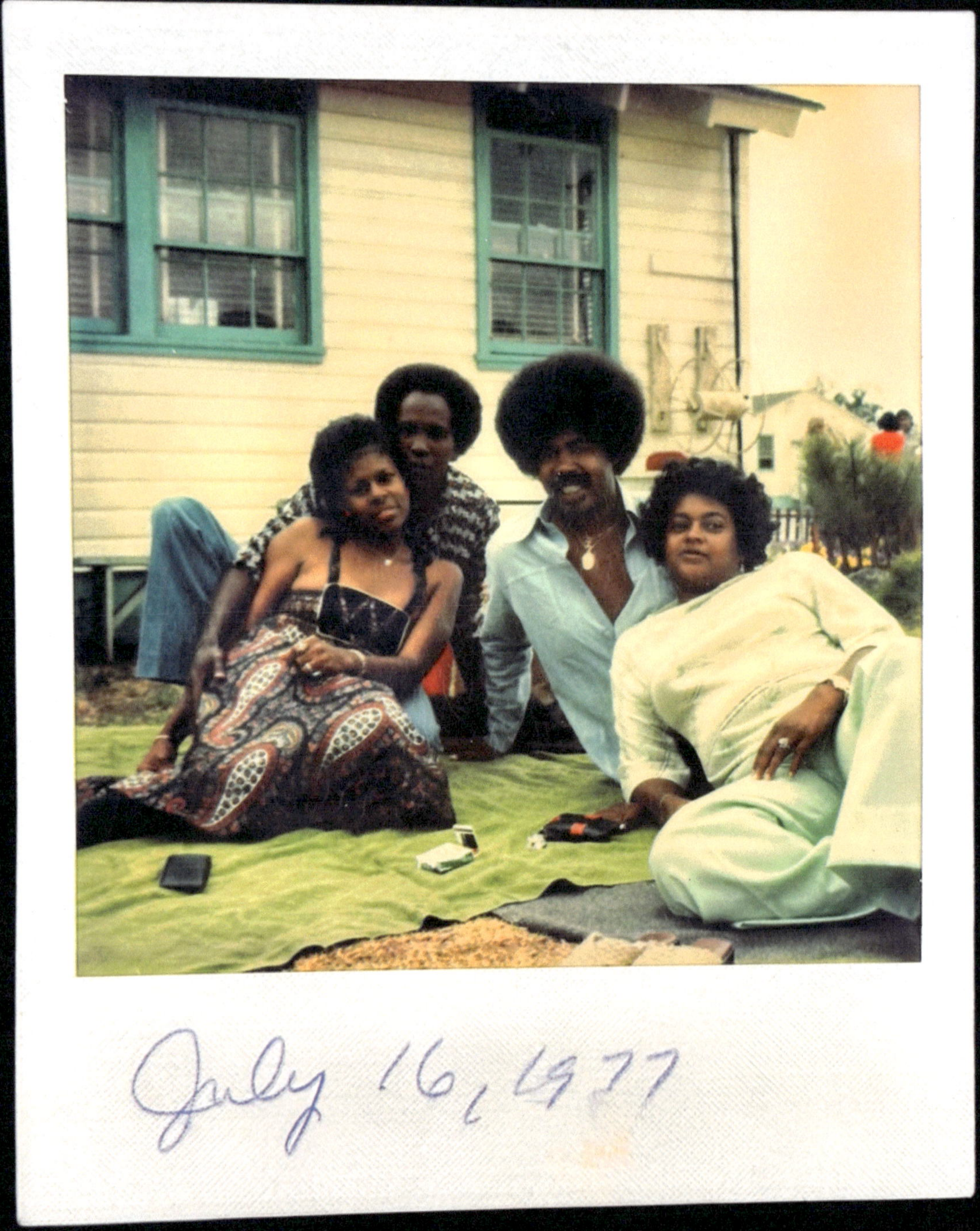

This picture was taken in the visiting area of California Men's Colony State Prison on July 16, 1977.

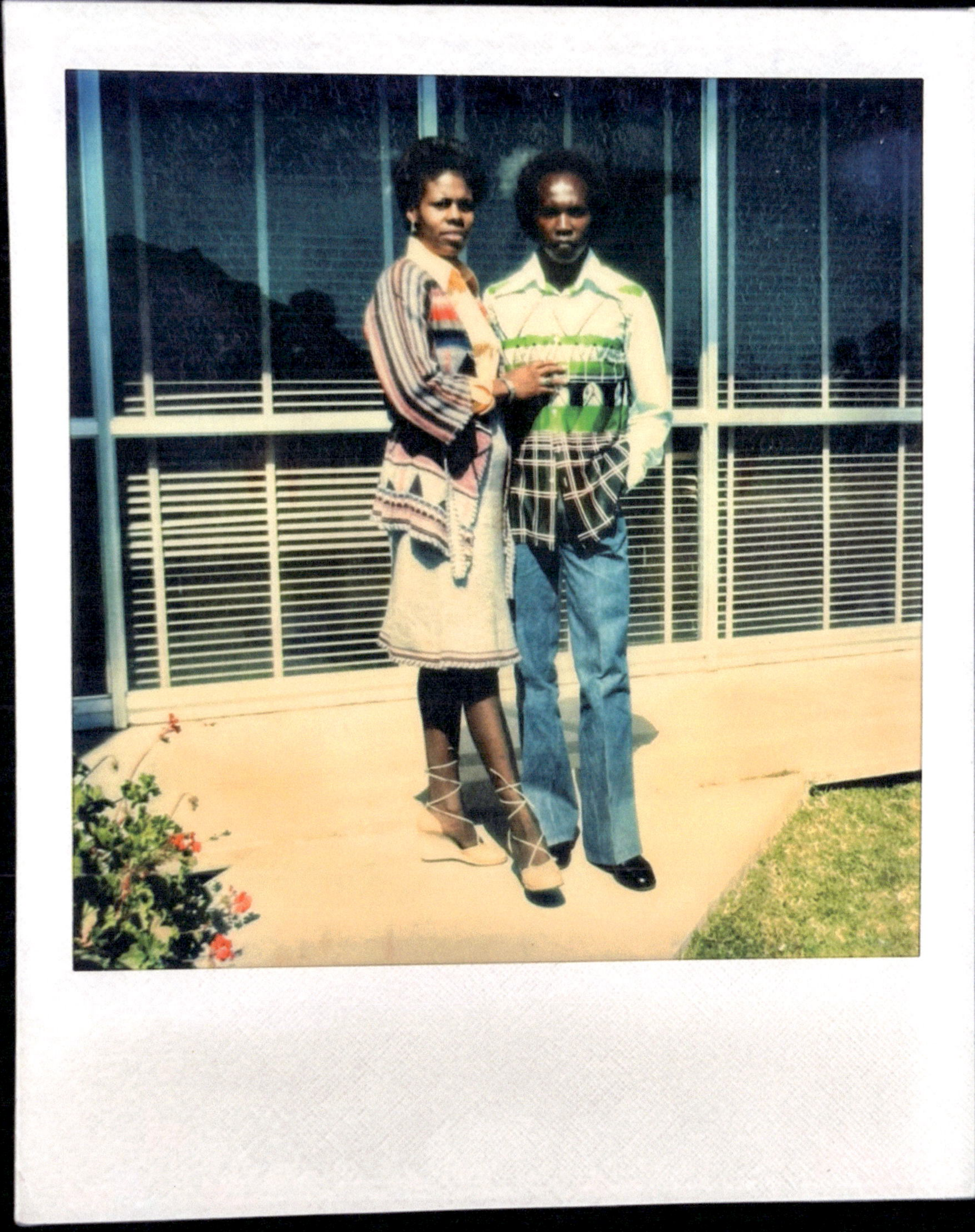

This picture was taken in the visiting area of California Men's Colony State Prison in

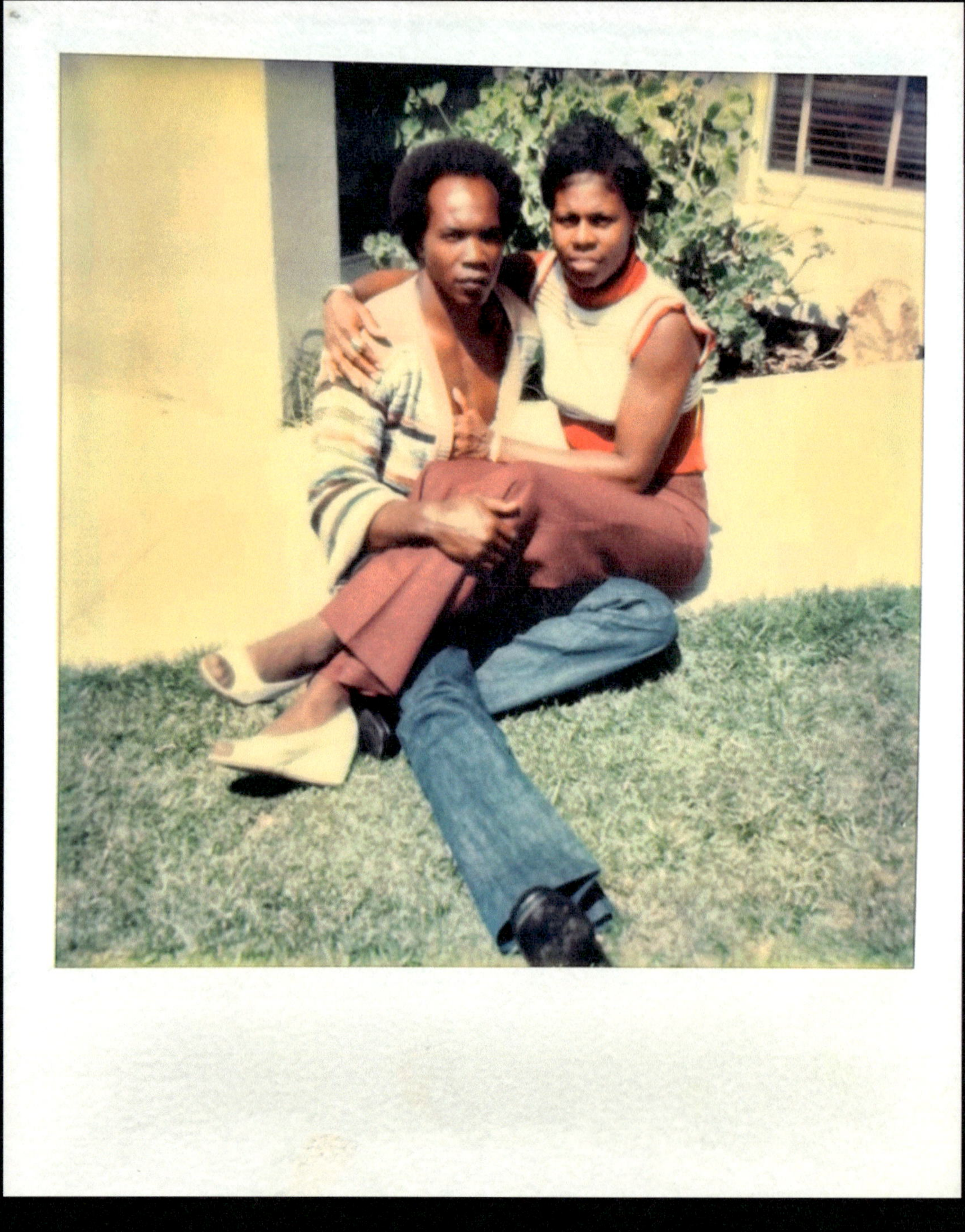

his picture was taken in the visiting area of California Men's Colony State Prison on
September 10, 1977.

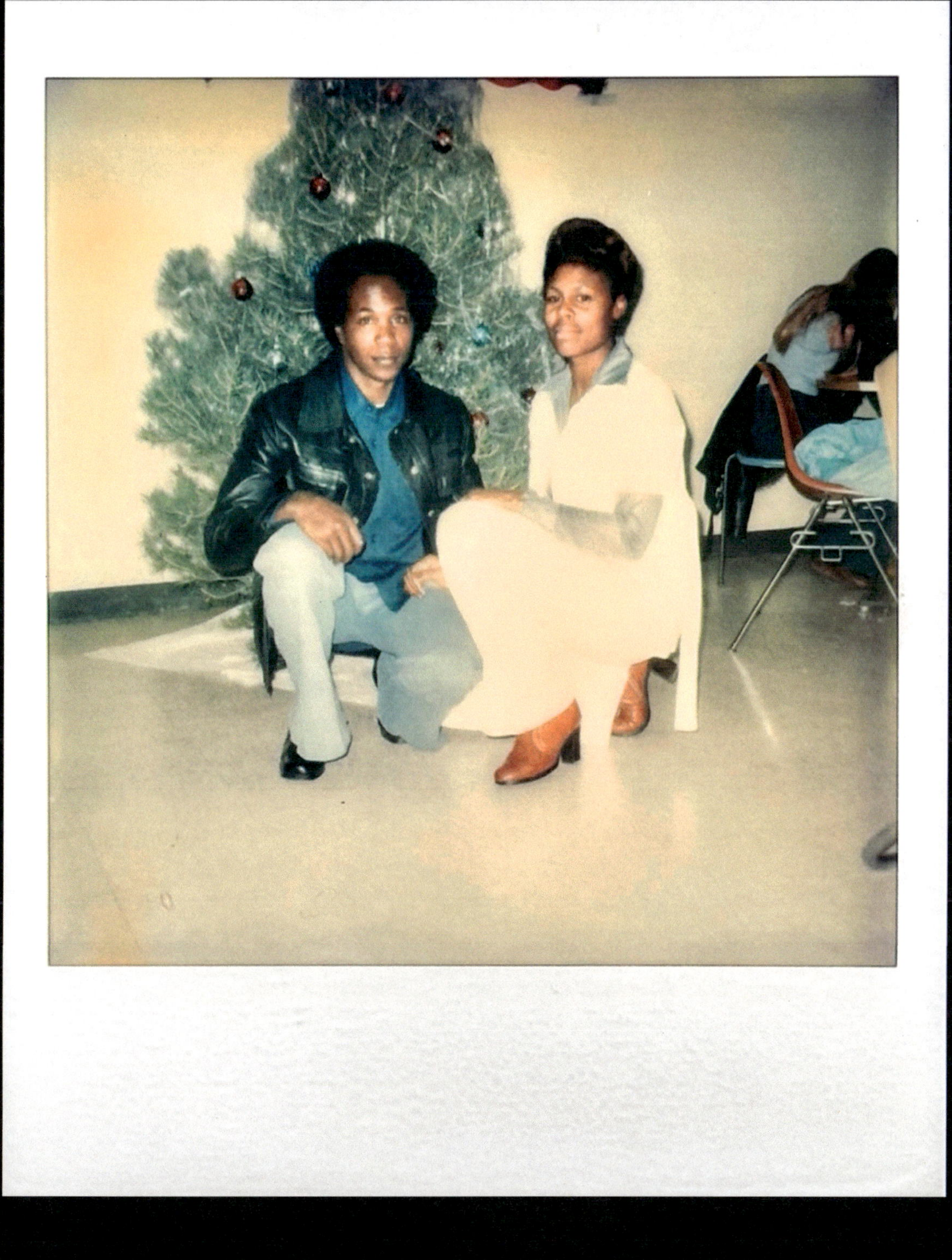

This picture was taken in the visiting area of Tehachapi State Prison on December 24
1977.

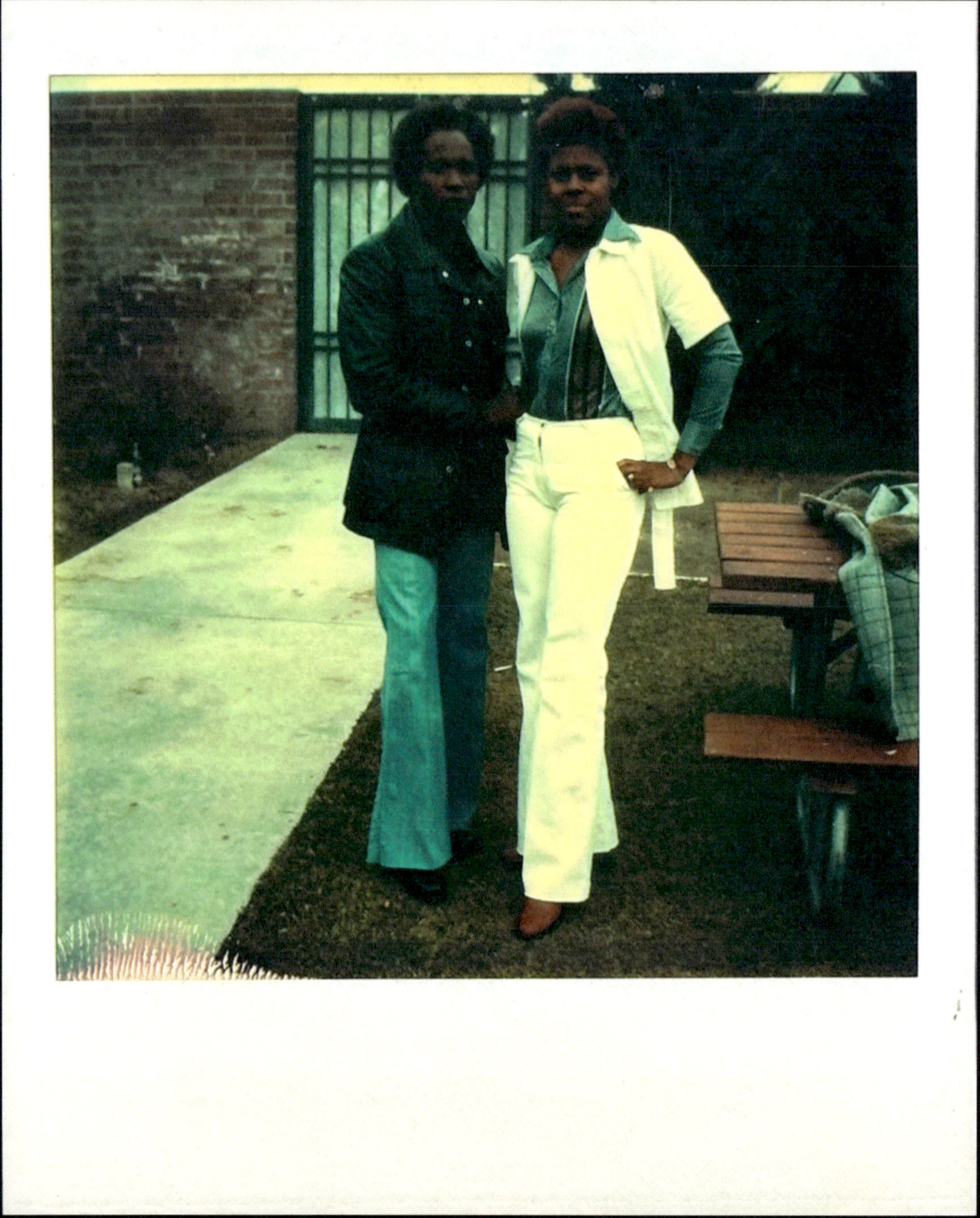

This picture was taken in the visiting area of Tehachapi State Prison on December 24, 1977.

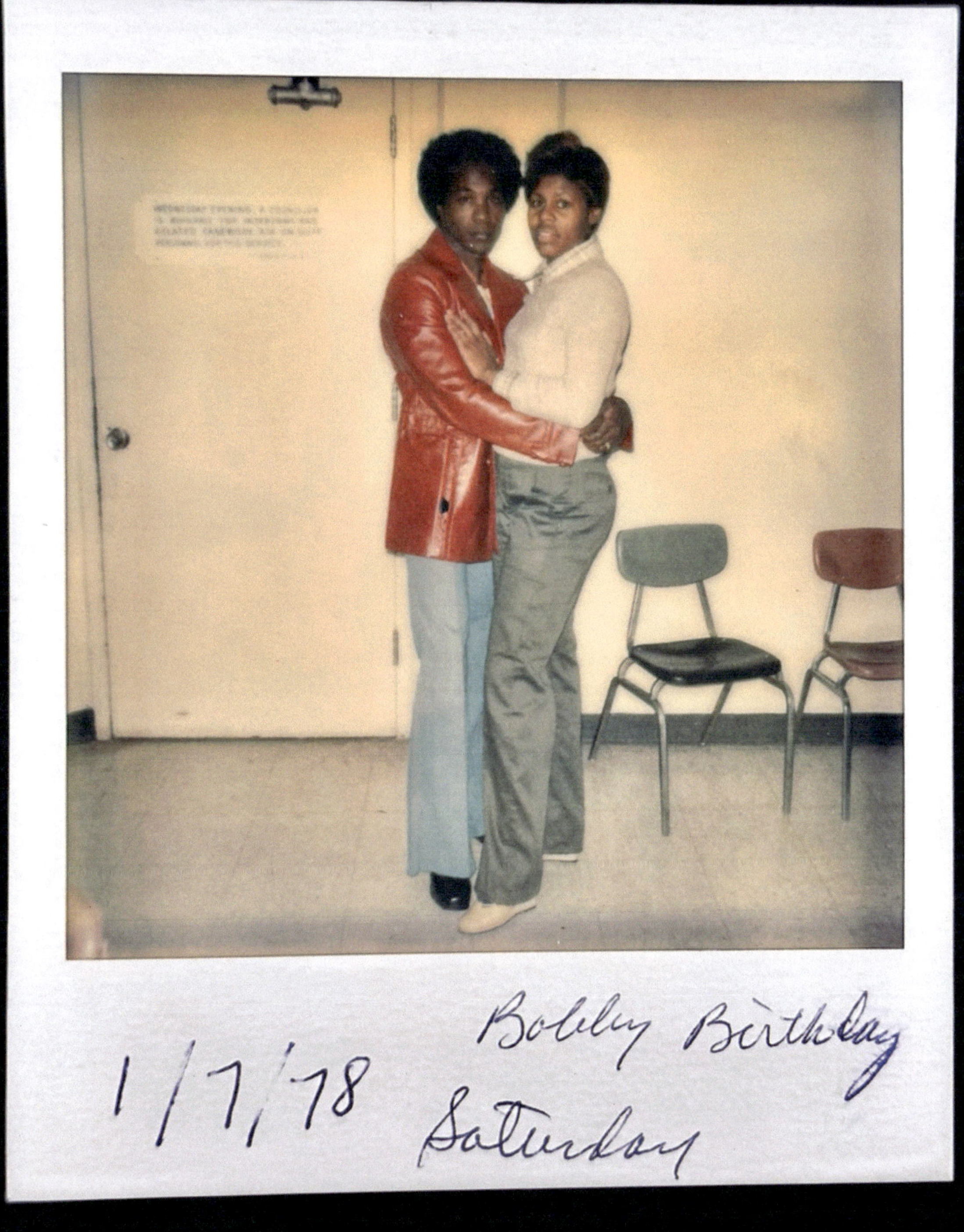

This picture was taken in the visiting area of Tehachapi State Prison on January 7, 1978

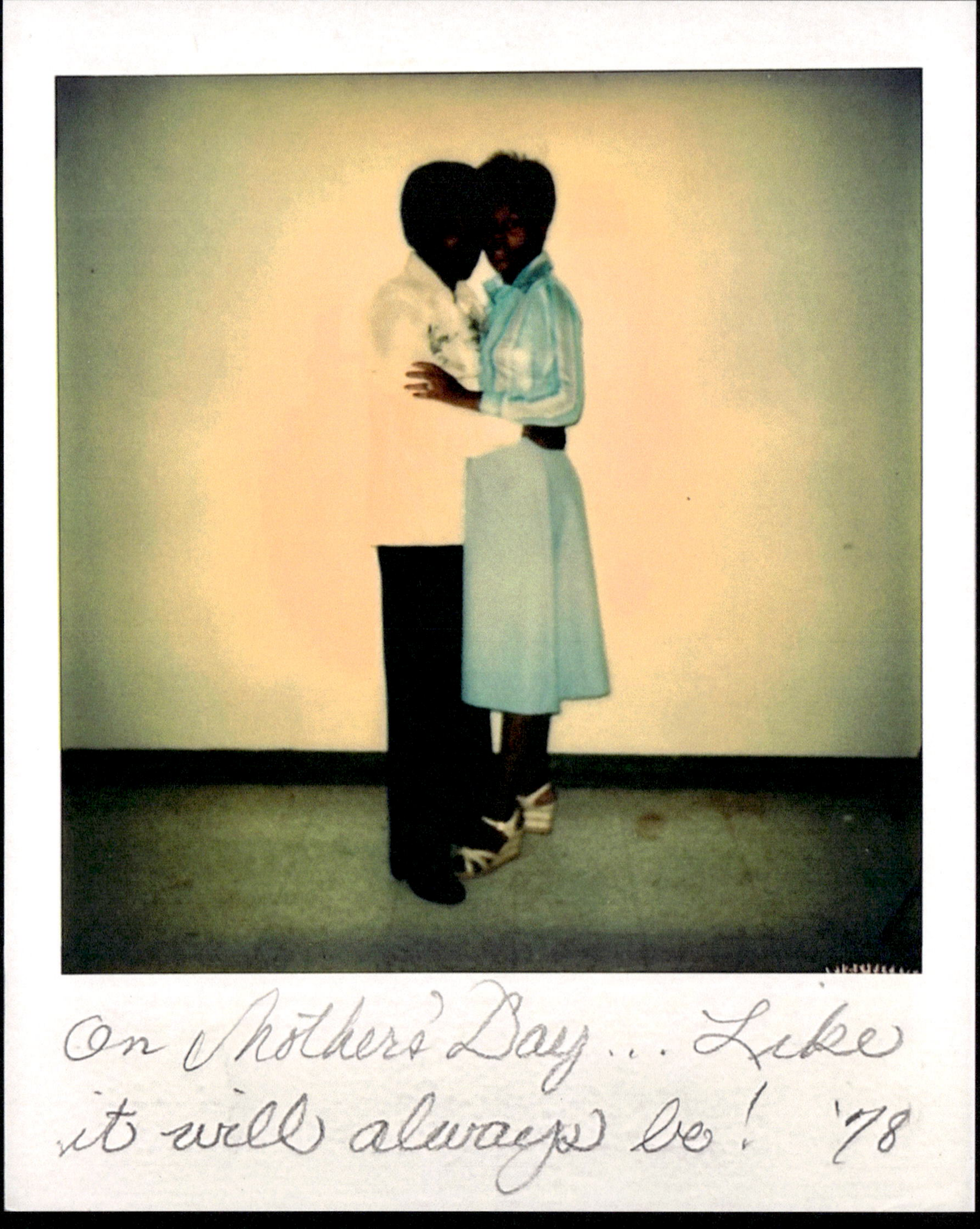

This picture was taken in the visiting area of Tehachapi State Prison on May 14, 1978

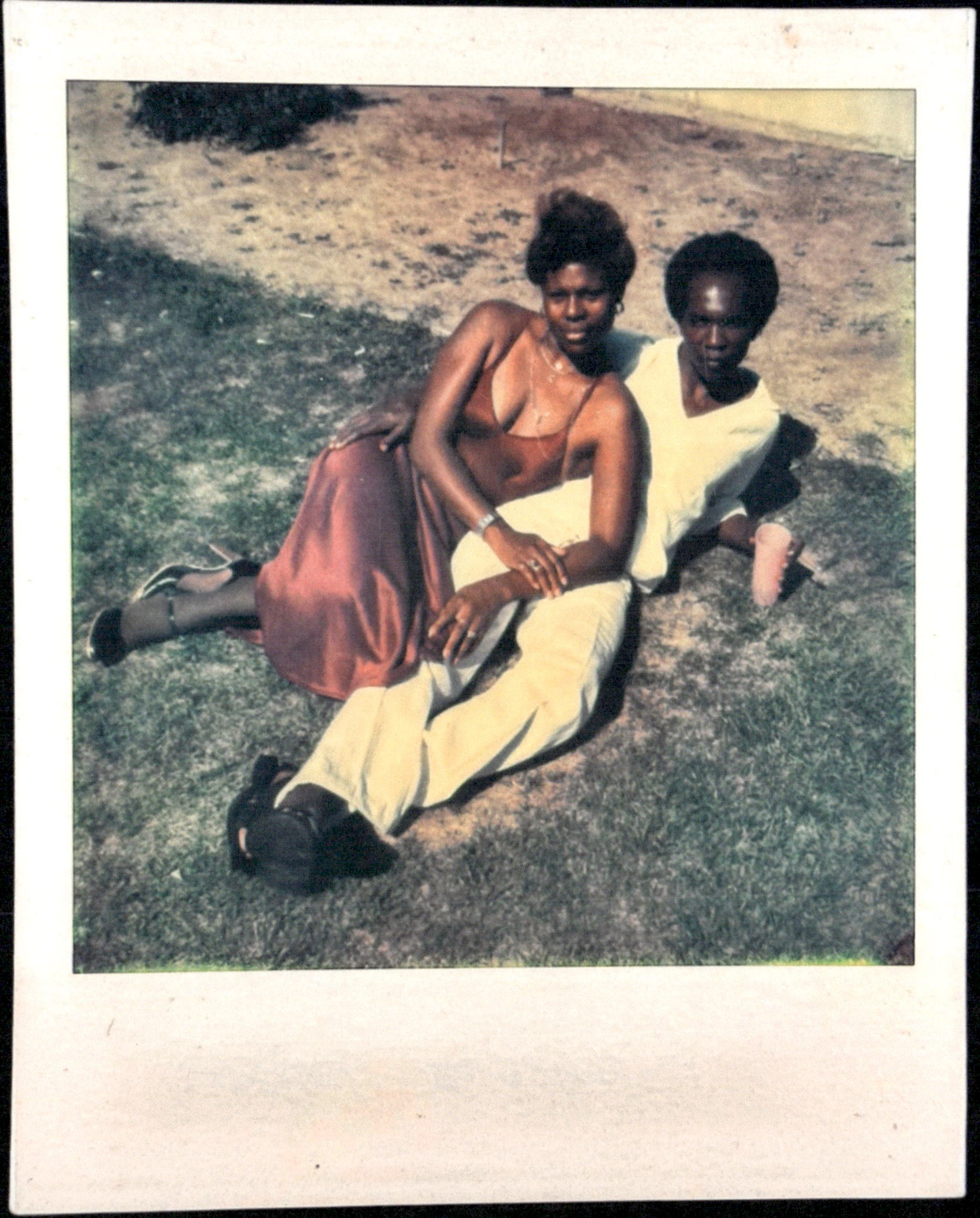

This picture was taken in the visiting area of Tehachapi State Prison on September 1, 1978

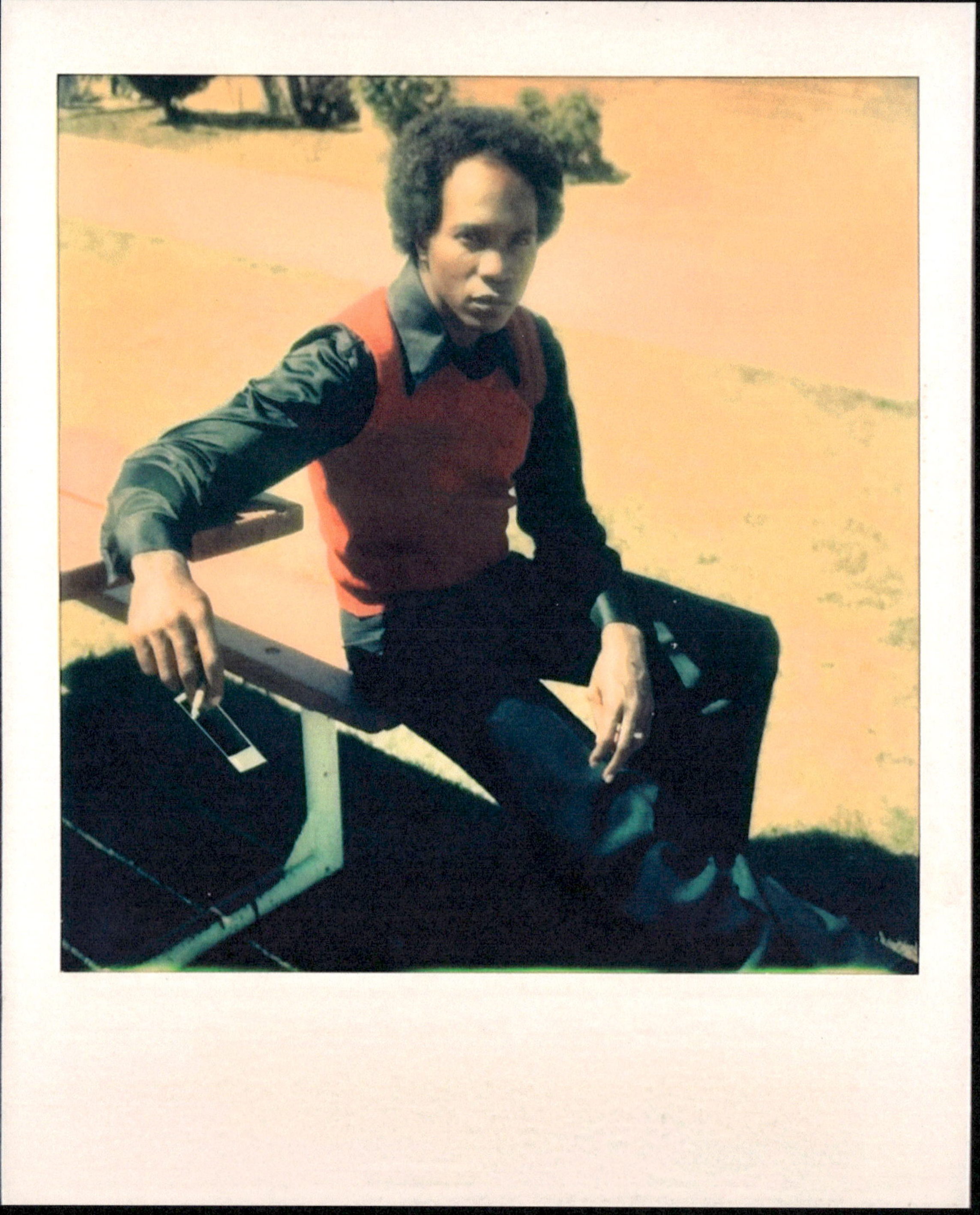

is picture was taken in the visiting area of Tehachapi State Prison on September 23, 1978.

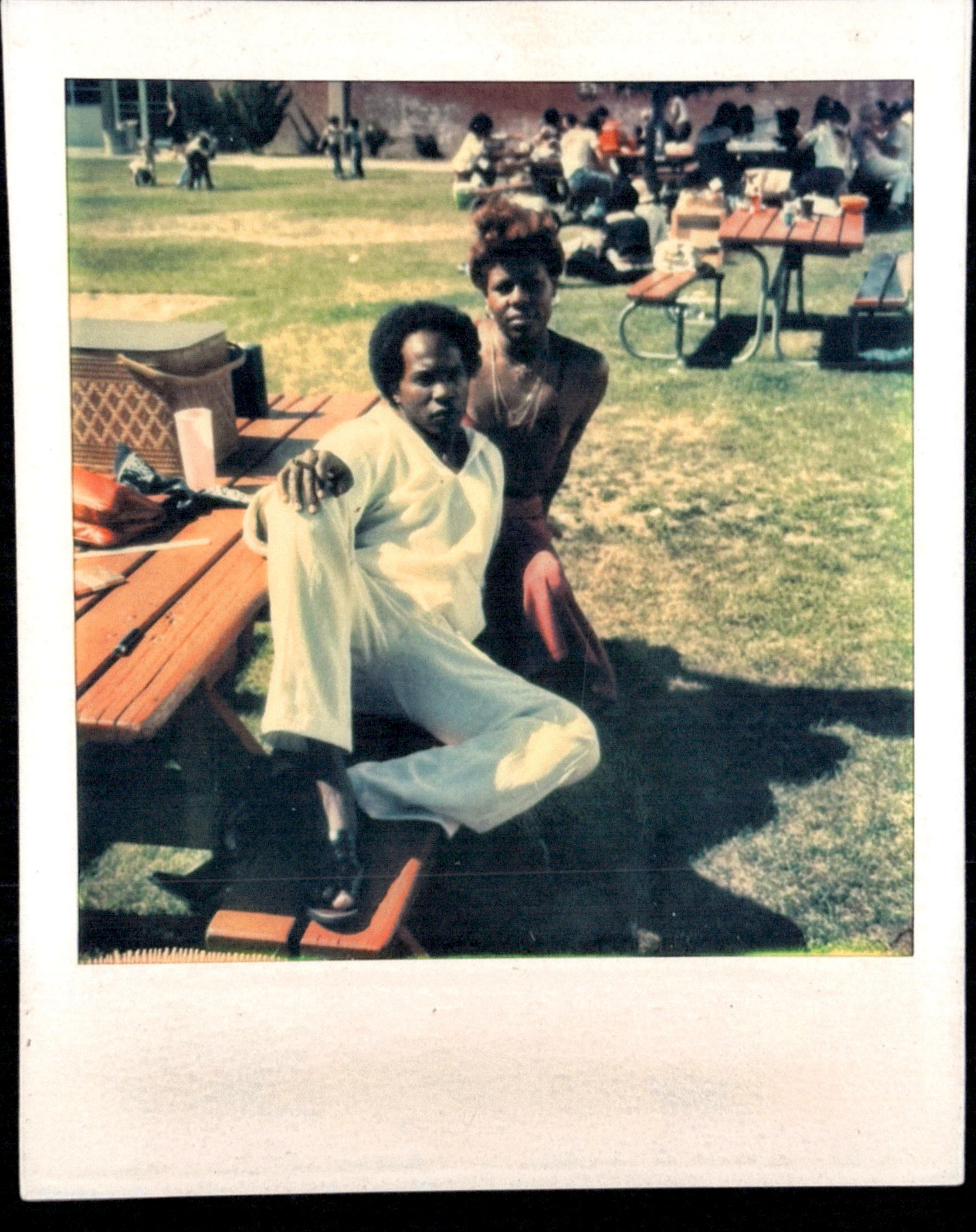

This picture was taken in the visiting area of Tehachapi State Prison on October 1, 1978.

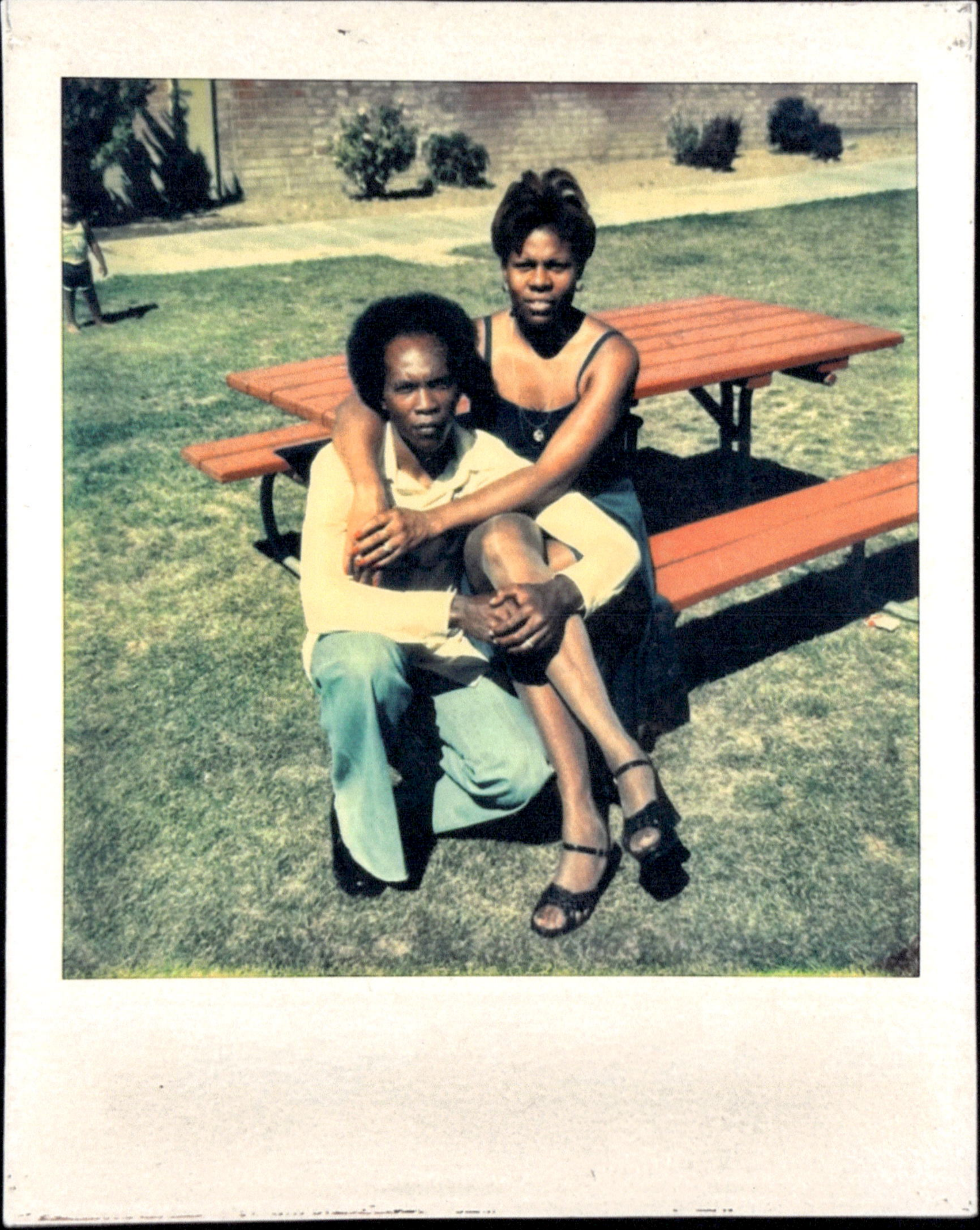

his picture was taken in the visiting area of Tehachapi State Prison on October 14, 197

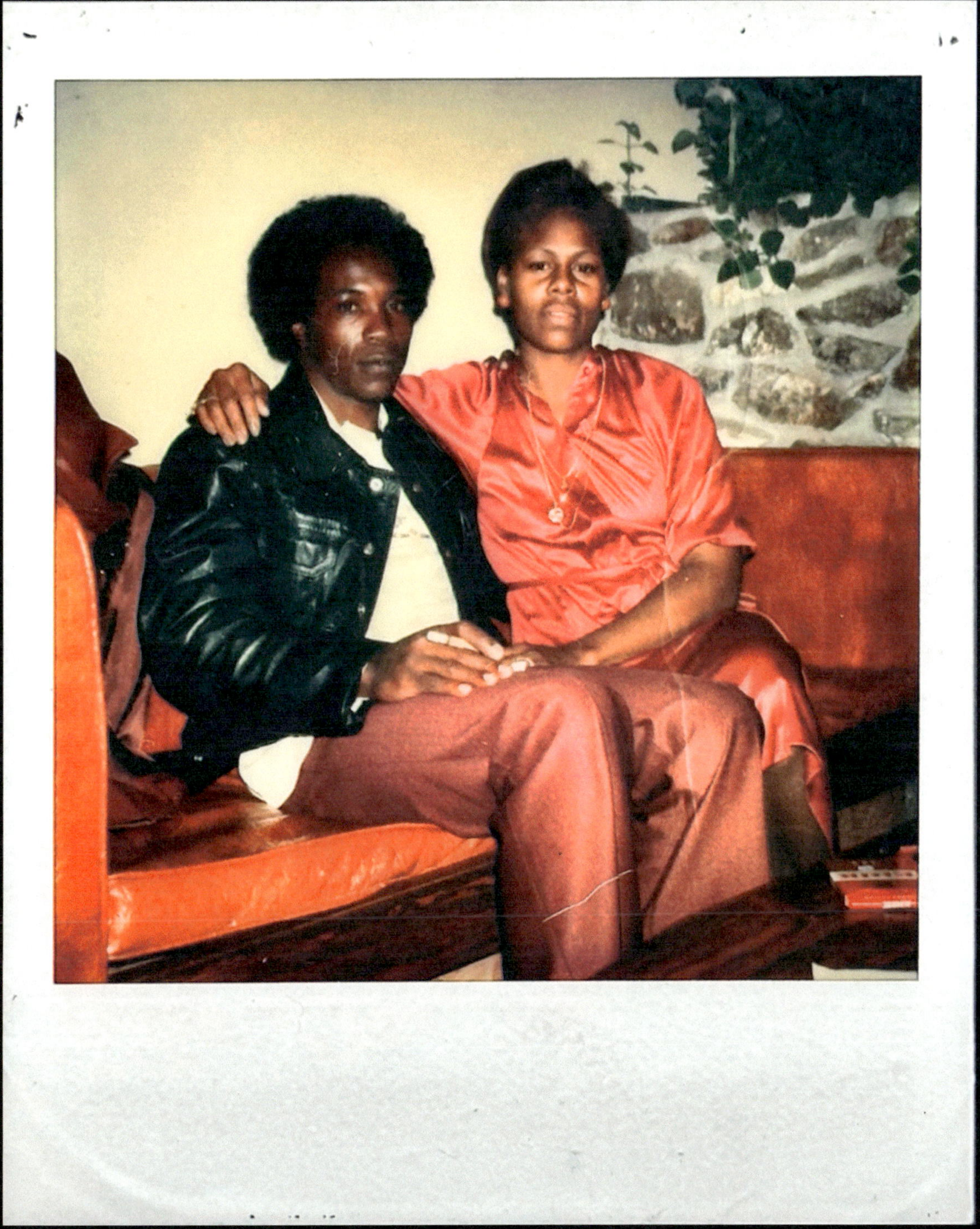

This picture was taken in the visiting area of Tehachapi State Prison on November 11, 1978.

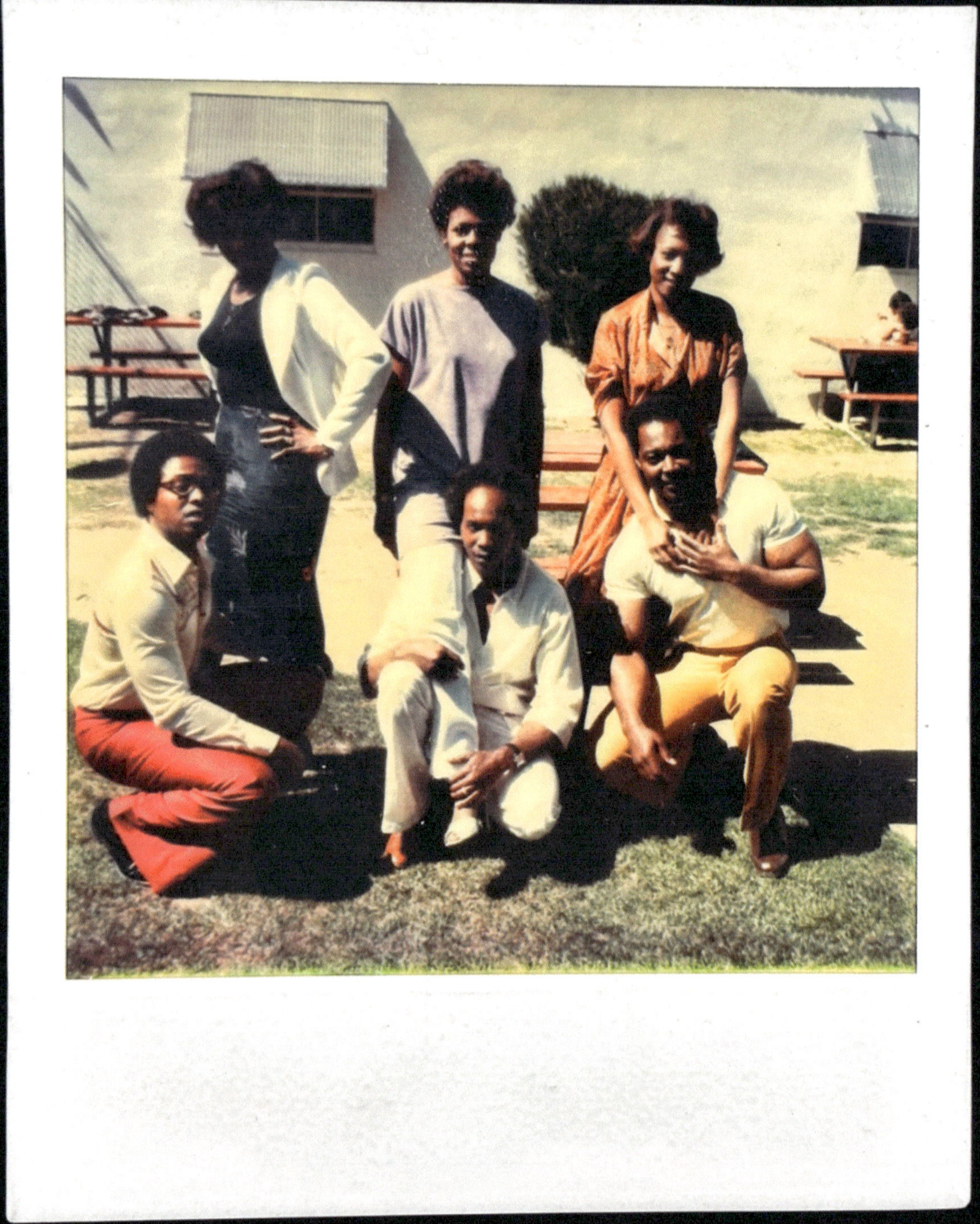

This picture was taken in the visiting area of Tehachapi State Prison in 1978.

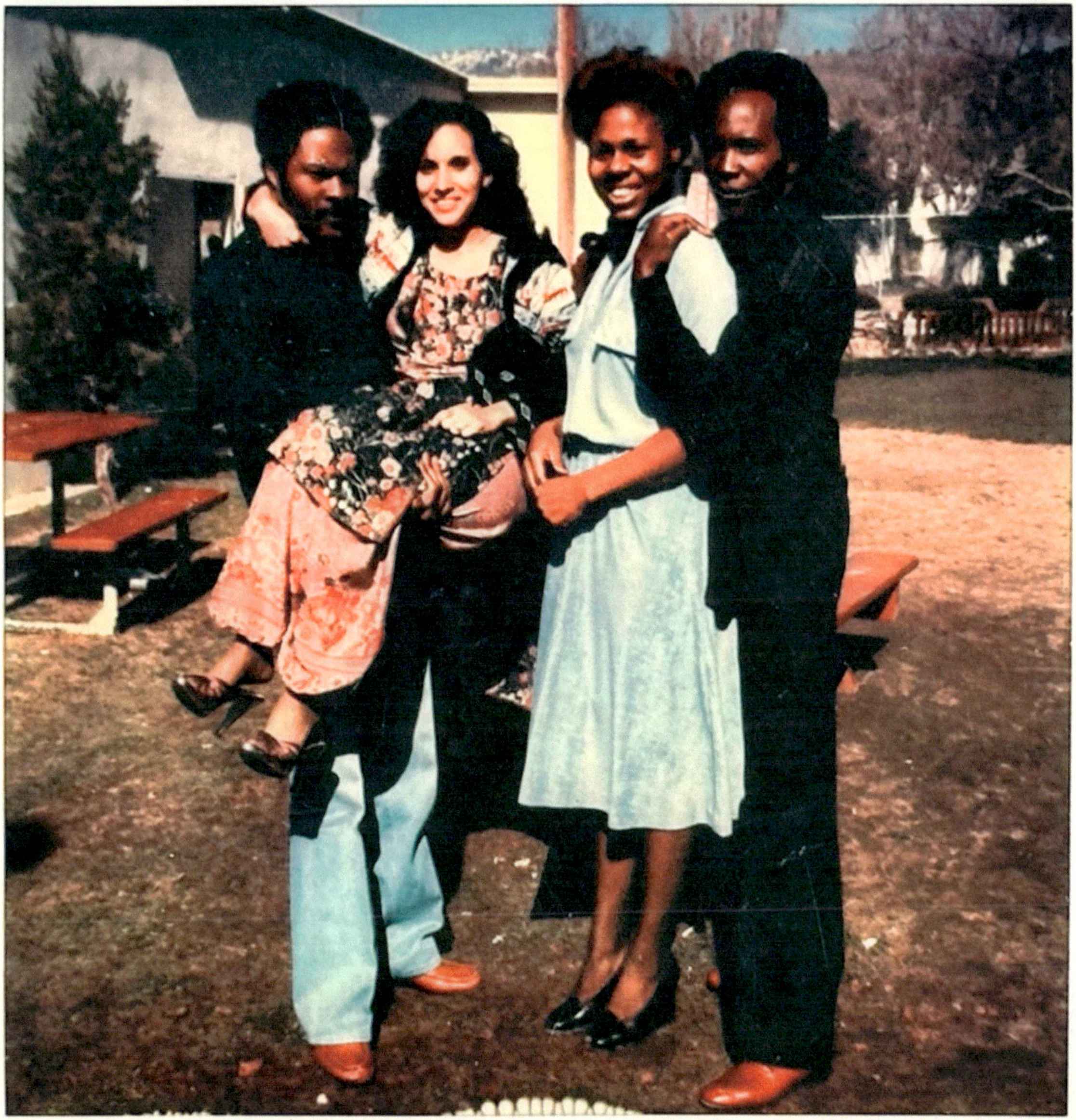

This picture was taken in the visiting area of Chino State Prison on March 3, 1979

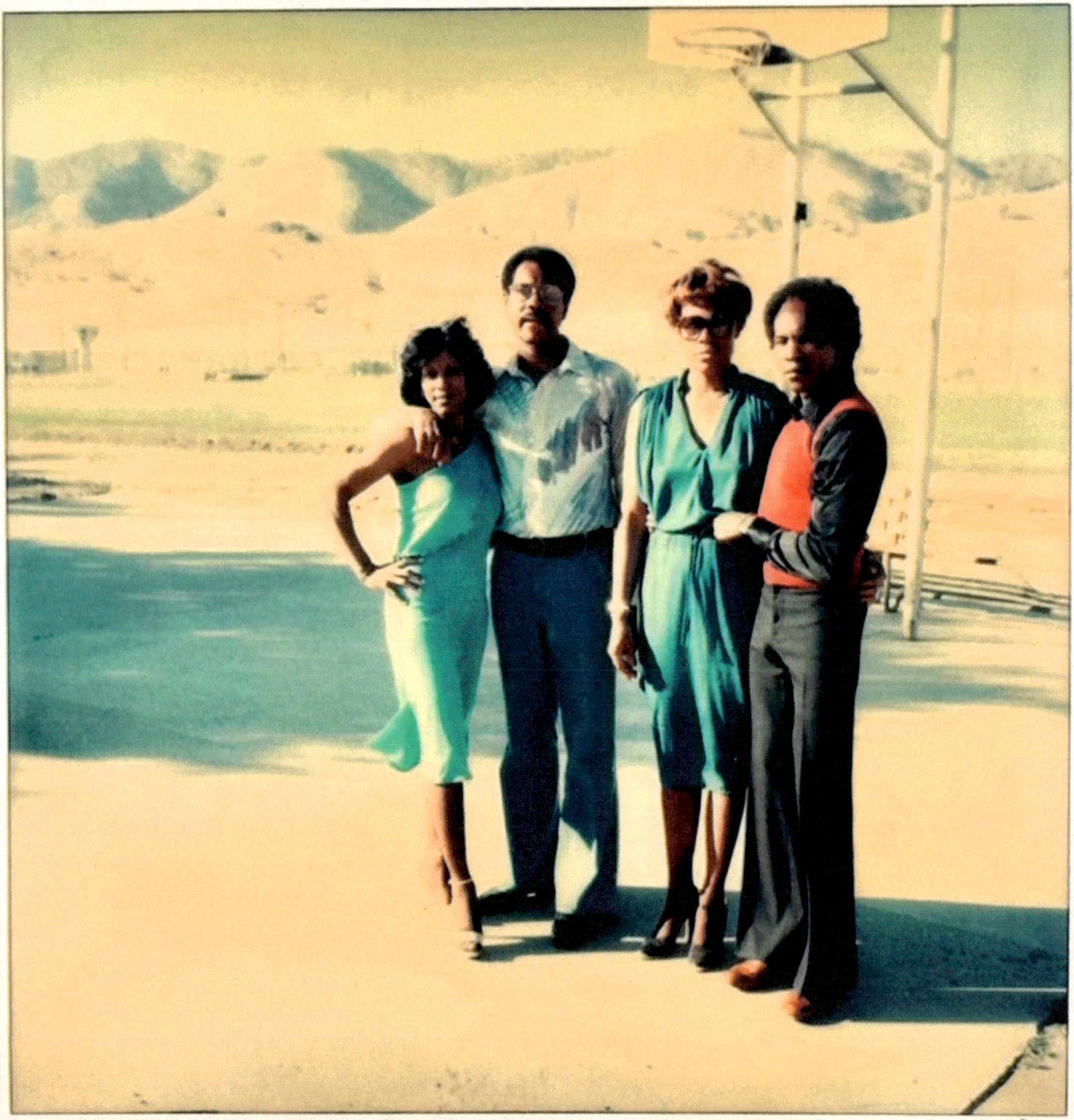

This picture was taken in the visiting area of Chino State Prison on June 30, 1979

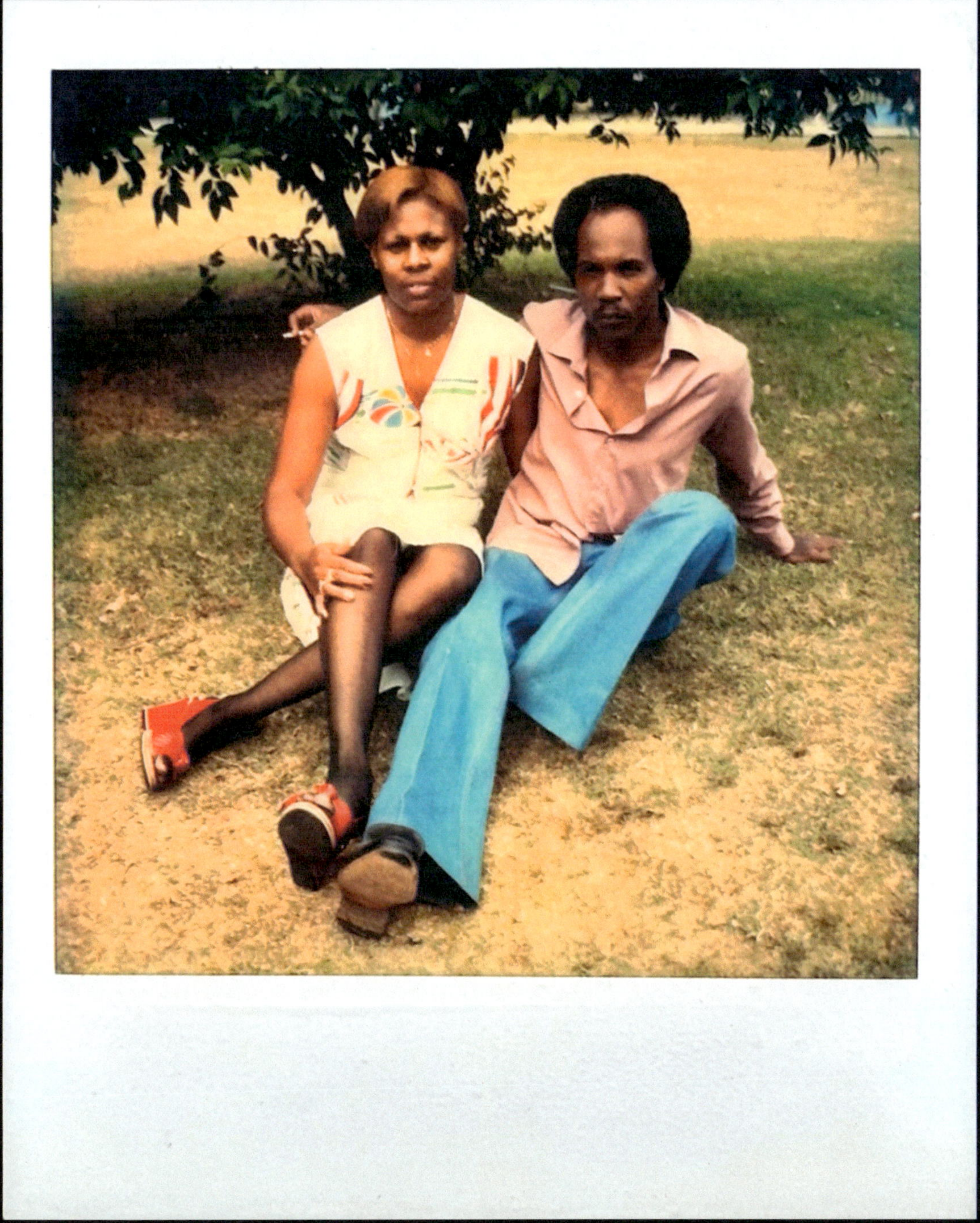

This picture was taken in the visiting area of Chino State Prison on October 25, 1980.

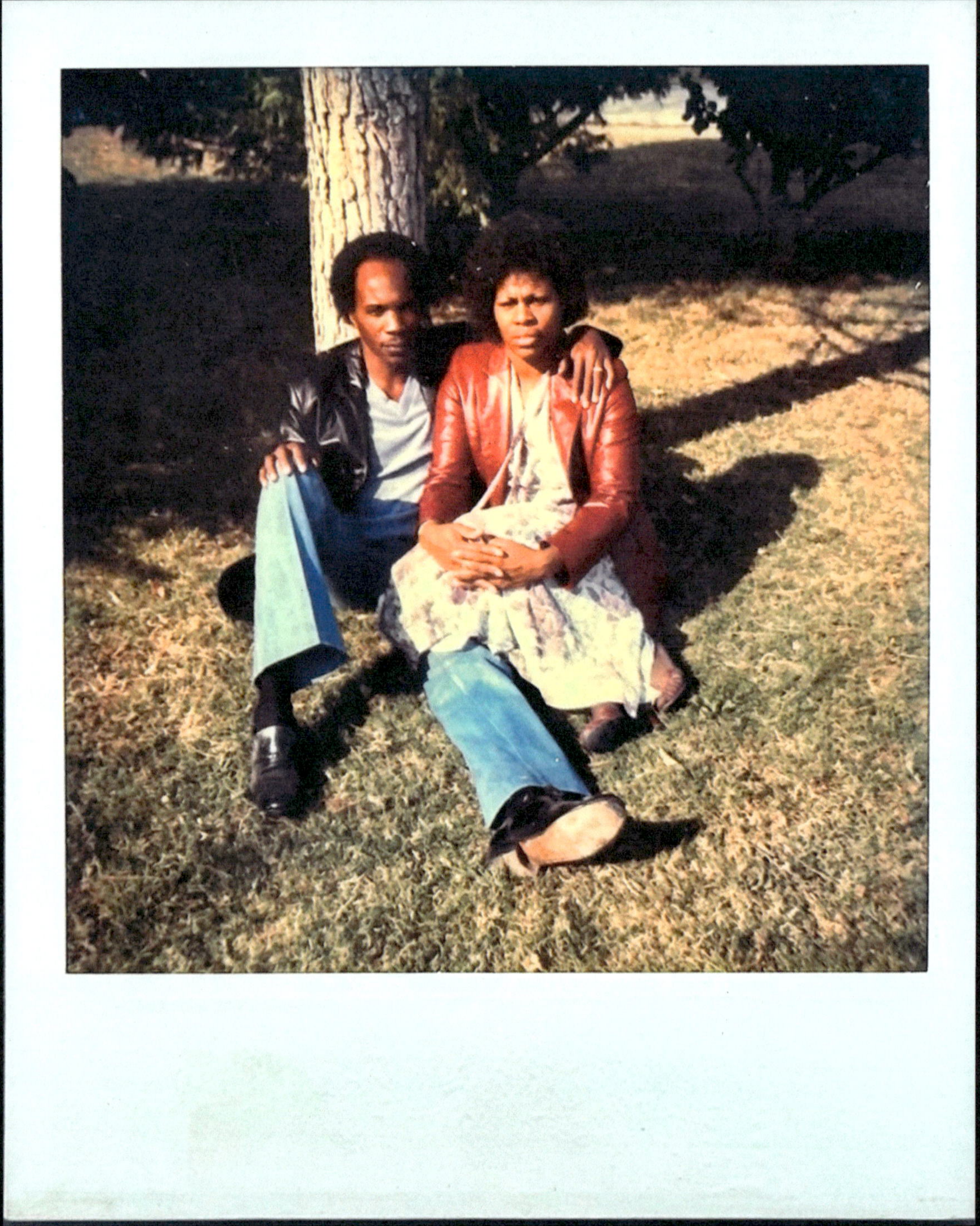

This picture was taken in the visiting area of Chino State Prison on November 29, 1980.

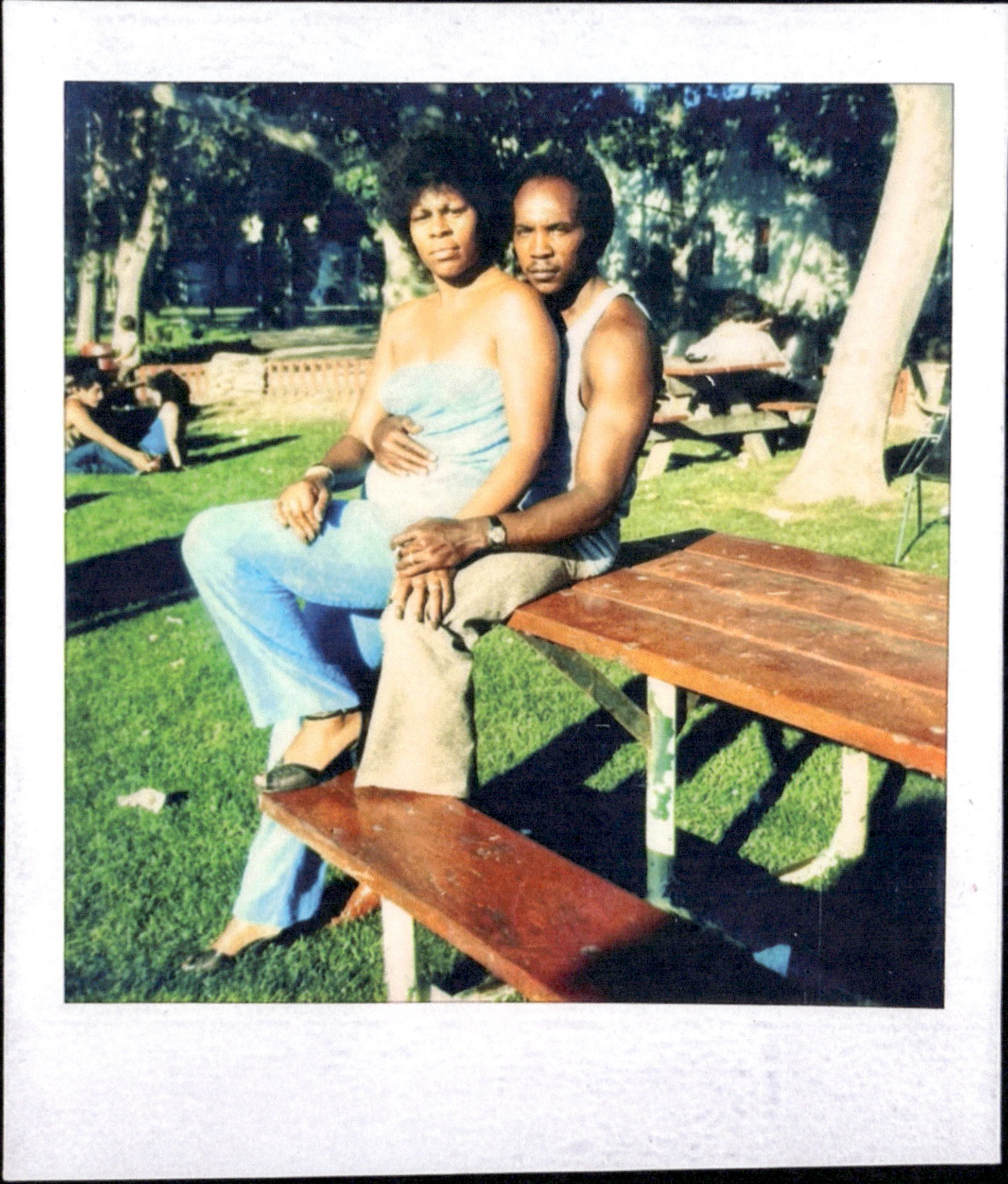

This picture was taken in the visiting area of Chino State Prison in 1980

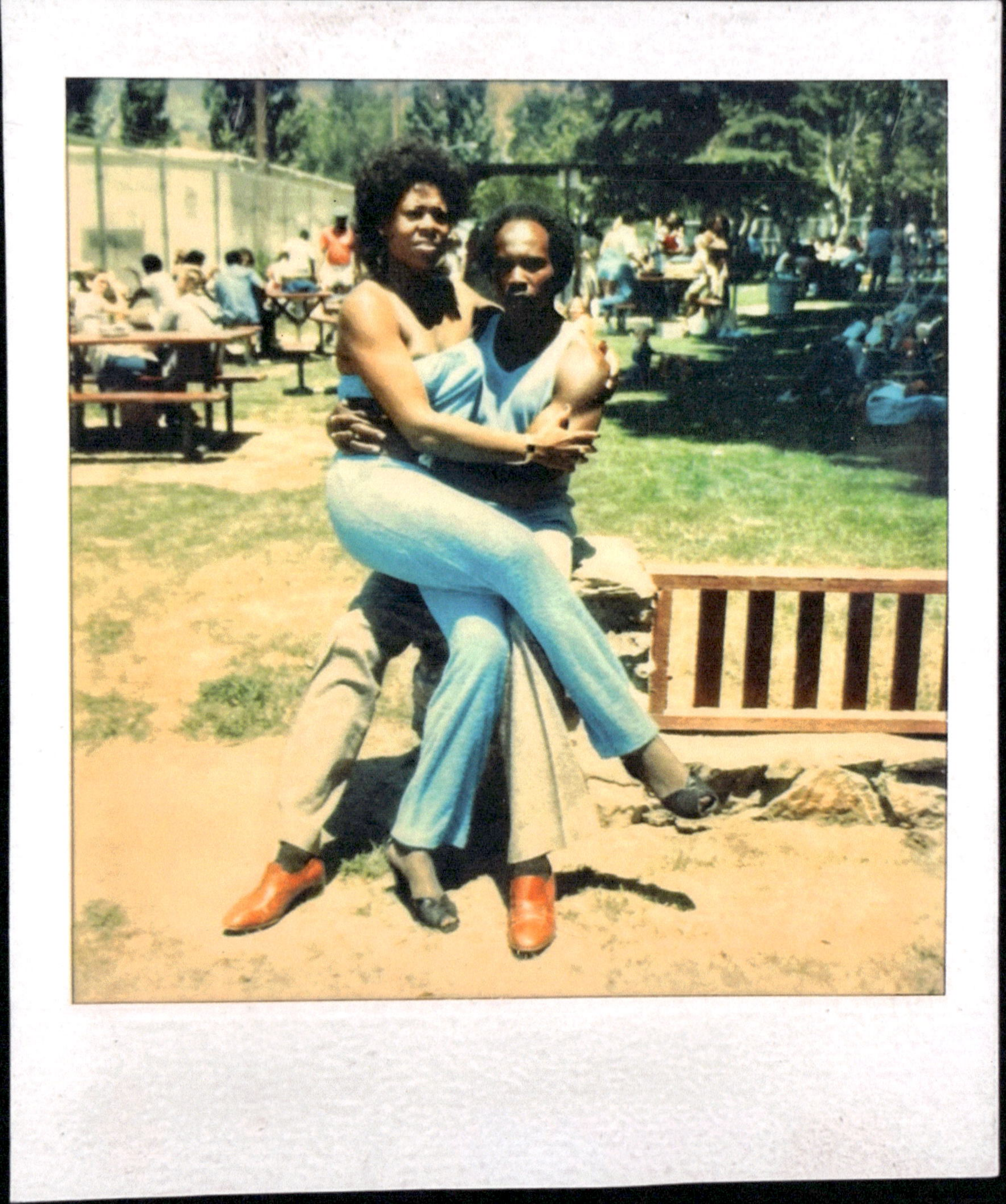

This picture was taken in the visiting area of Chino State Prison in 1980.

About the Author

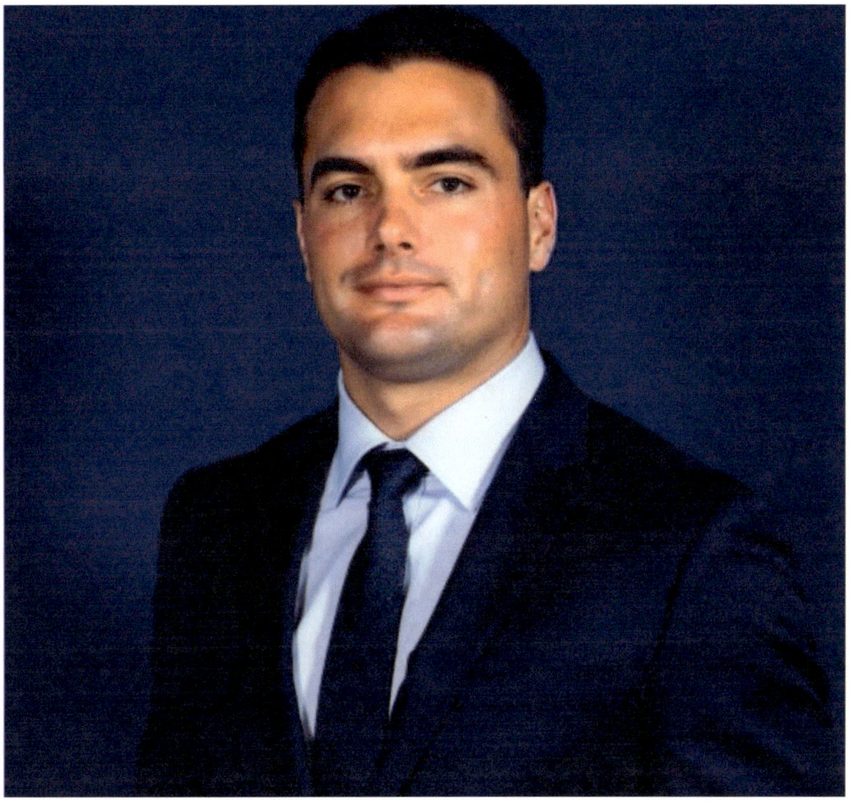

Eric has emerged as a highly accomplished investor and Day Trader, engaging in trading activities with a substantial value of stocks annually. He enjoys the status of a dedicated husband and father, being blessed with four wonderful daughters who hold a special place in his heart. Eric's existence revolves around upholding the virtues of a devout Christian, a devoted husband, and a caring father guided by the grace of God. His journey has been transformative, considering his challenging upbringing, and he now stands as an illustrious testament to the boundless possibilities achievable through faith in God.

Eric joined a criminal street gang as a teenager, and he was eventually arrested and put in a cage at the Long Beach City Jail. He dropped out of Jordan High School in Long Beach, California, in the 10th grade. Eric eventually got on the right path by the grace of God and obtained his GED the same month that he would have graduated. He joined the United States Coast Guard at 18, and after four years of faithful service, he was honorably discharged.

The following is an excerpt from his autobiography: "California Prison Confessions." "It was a typical beautiful summer night in Long Beach, California, and the three young teens fighting in the musty garage starkly contrasted the night's serenity. A teen called Bones was thrown against a wall, and a muscular teenager nicknamed E Double (me) rushed towards him and violently punched him in his lower back. Another youth named Tim Loc held Bones against the wall during this attack. E Double's knuckles landed with a thick-sounding thud as Bones grimaced and moaned in pain from each successive blow.

There's a look of pain and fear in Bone's eyes as E Double mercilessly lands blow after blow to his kidneys. E Double has spent years hitting the heavy bag in his garage, so his punches are devastating for his age. The beating lasted a minute, and the two teens stopped attacking the unfortunate victim. Amazingly, they all shook hands and embraced each other. We were all friends, and this was our modest gang initiation into our small clique called 'Six Feet Under.'"

Our tiny neighborhood gang in North Long Beach, California, had several members of various races: White, Black, and Hispanic. The definition of a criminal street gang according to the California Penal Code is as follows: "As used in this chapter, 'criminal street gang' means any ongoing organization, association, or group of three or more persons, whether formal or informal, having as one of its primary activities the commission of one or more of the criminal acts…having a common name or common identifying sign or symbol, and whose members individually or collectively engage in or have engaged in a pattern of criminal gang activity," California Penal Code 186.22(f).

Some of our associates committed serious crimes such as burglaries, drug sales, stealing cars, carrying guns, vandalism, and assaulting people. Although we were nothing but young punks, we were a criminal street gang according to the California Penal Code.

The FBI did a study entitled "Street-Gang Mentality: A Mosaic of Remorseless Violence and Relentless Loyalty." I want to quote a relevant part concerning young males who do not have a father or other positive male role models in their lives while growing up: "All gang members lacked male role models in their households, and when they lived with their mothers, they were rarely home because of work schedules. Gang members often lived temporarily with various people. All but one gang member reported that one or more immediate family members had a criminal history or abused drugs. Gangs attracted them because of their loyalty, stability, and sense of group identity."

There is an epidemic in this country of boys masquerading as men who don't take their responsibilities as fathers seriously. Many fathers aren't involved in their children's lives; if they are, they are a horrible example of what a real man should be. One of the main factors in young men ending up in the penal system is the lack of a father or, at the very least, a positive male role model when they were growing up. Absentee fathers are causing society to pay a high price for their selfish and callous actions.

Every day, I strive to be the best dad to the four beautiful daughters God has blessed me with. I live by the motto, "Be the man you needed as a child." I will not allow the actions of physically and emotionally abusive people to define who I am or hinder my advancement in life. You can choose to be bitter or better. I strive for excellence because living well is the best response to abusive people.

Eric Sturgess

God bless you and yours.

Romans 10:9-13

For those seeking to connect with Eric or gather additional insights about his upcoming projects, please visit his official website: EricSturgess.com.

Other Books

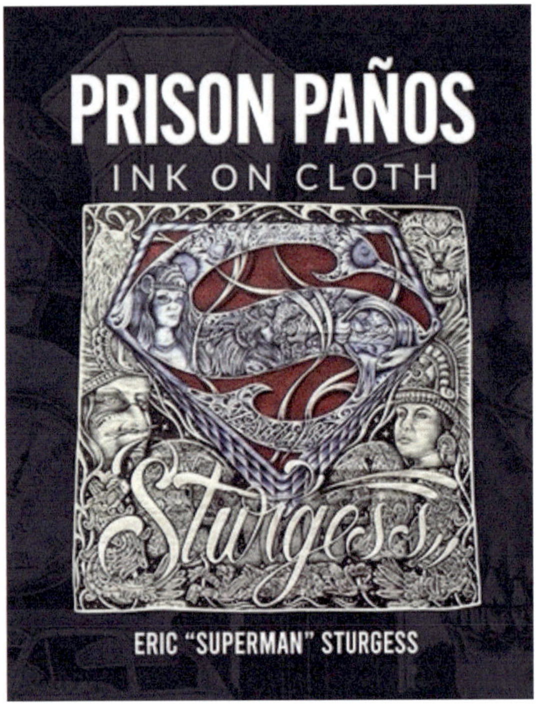

Prison Paños: Ink On Cloth

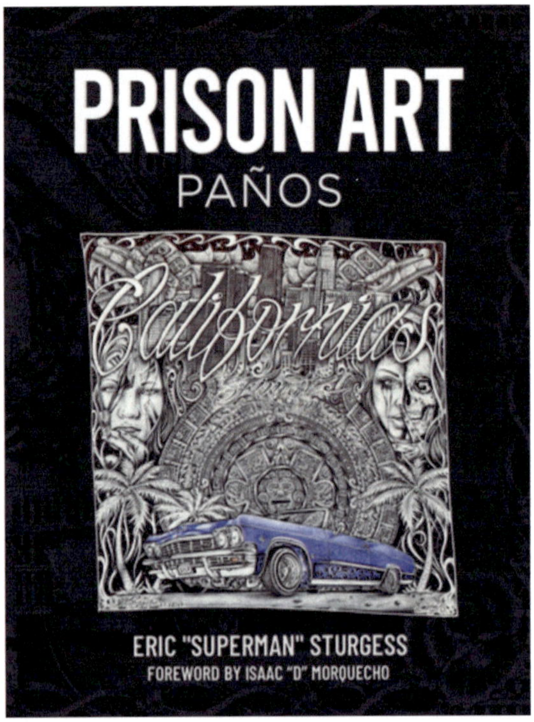

Prison Art Paños

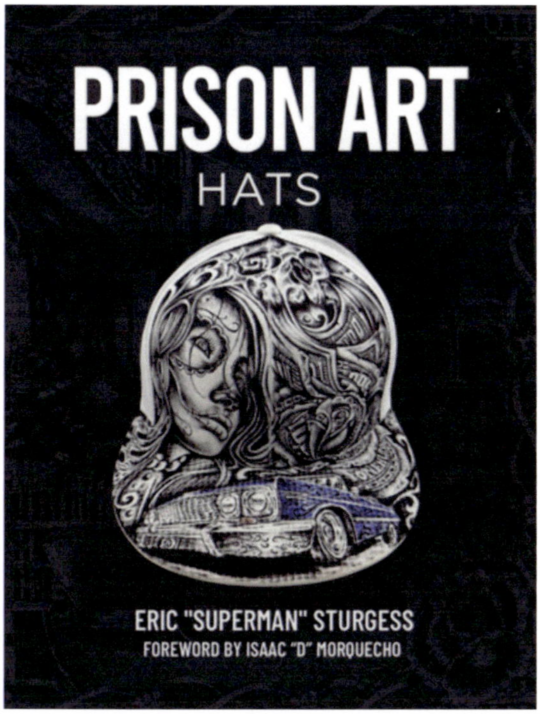

Prison Art Hats

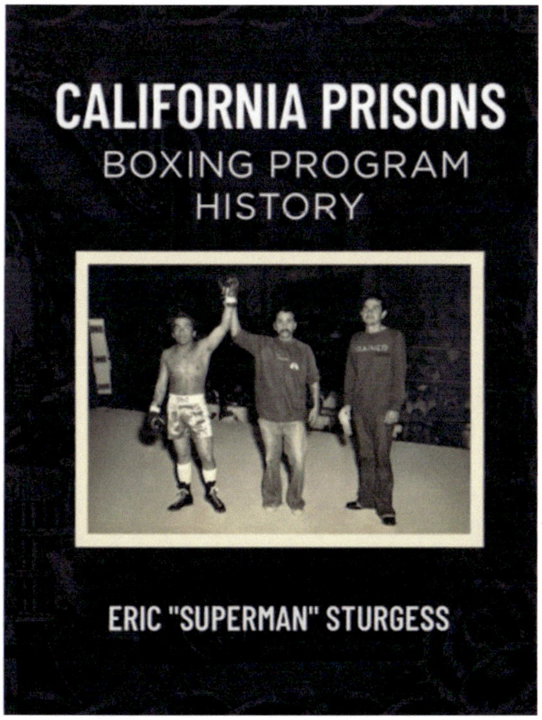

California Prisons: Boxing Program History

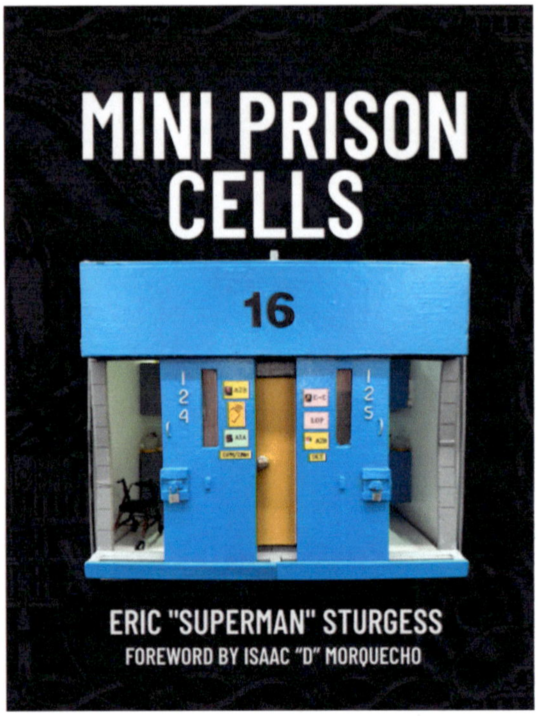

Mini Prison Cells

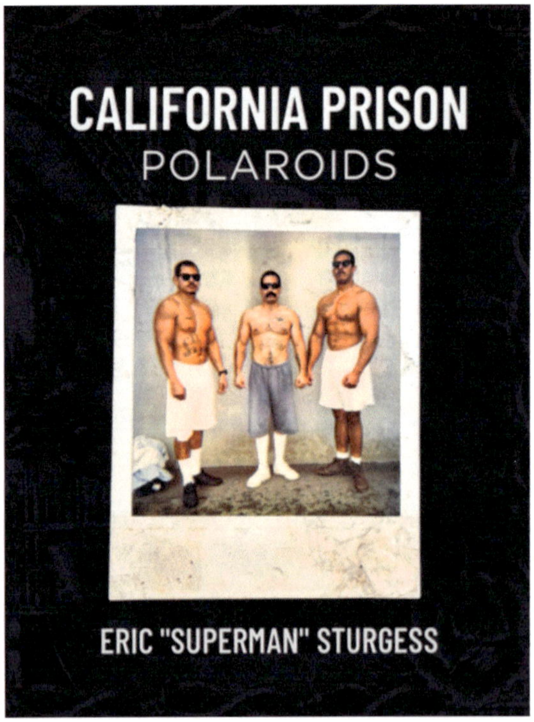

California Prison Polaroids

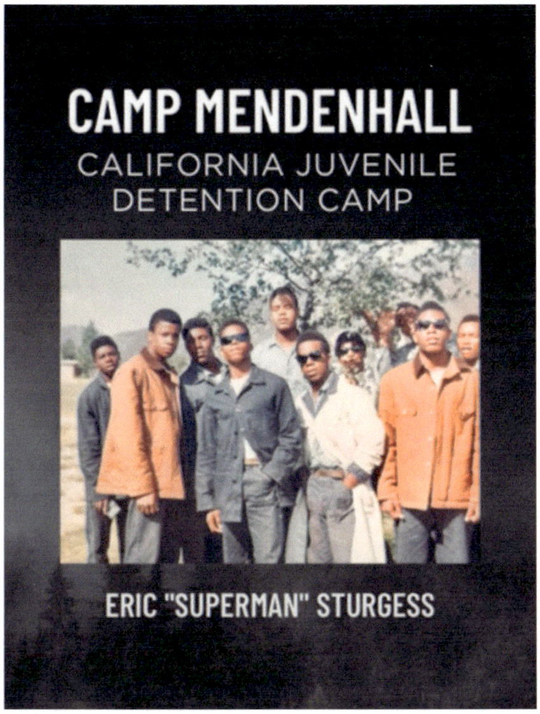

Camp Mendenhall: California Juvenile Detention Camp

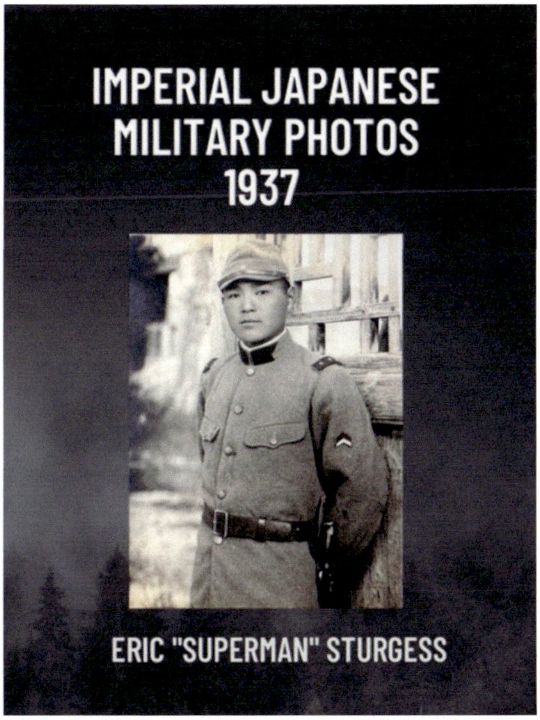

Imperial Japanese Military Photos 1937

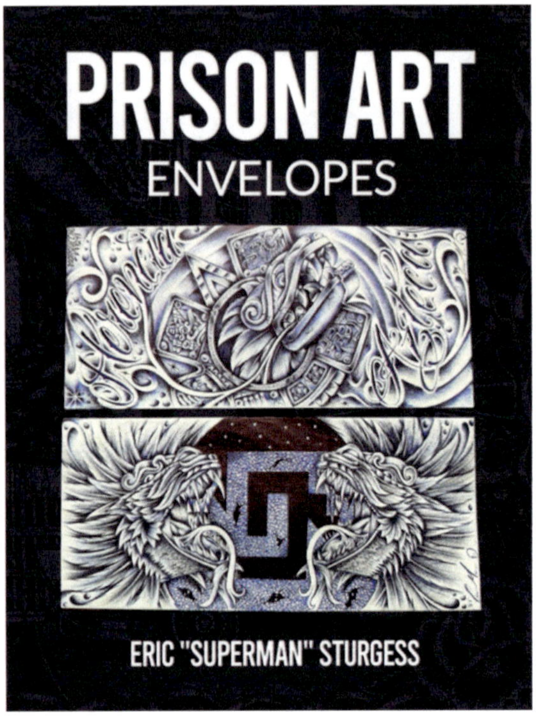

Prison Art Envelopes

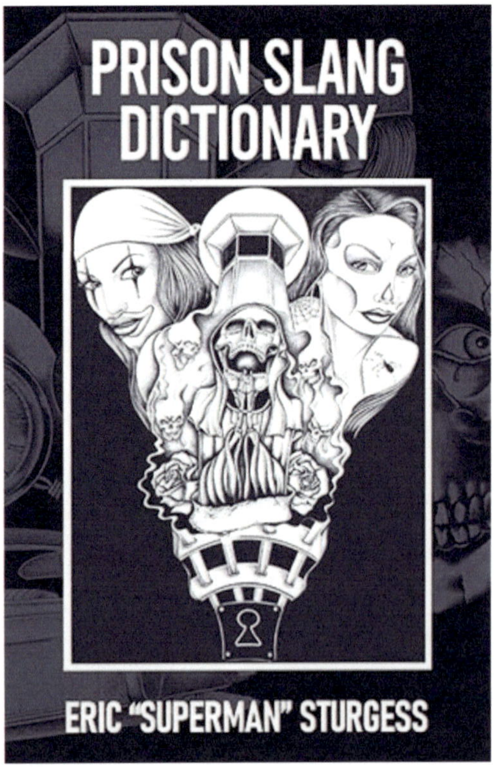

Prison Slang Dictionary

Made in the USA
Monee, IL
05 November 2026

67378692R00040